THE
ESSENCE OF MAN

AHMED HULUSI

As with all my works, this book is not copyrighted.
As long as it remains faithful to the original,
it may be freely printed, reproduced, published and translated.
For the knowledge of ALLAH, there is no recompense.

Copyright © 2012 **Ahmed Hulusi**
All rights reserved.
ISBN-10: 0615725244
ISBN-13: 978-0615725246

THE
ESSENCE of MAN

AHMED HULUSI

www.ahmedhulusi.org/en/

Translated by ALIYA ATALAY

ABOUT THE COVER

The black background of the front cover represents darkness and ignorance, while the white color of the letters represents light and knowledge.

The image is a Kufi calligraphy of the Word of Unity: *"La ilaha illallah; Muhammad Rasulullah"* which means,

"There is no concept such as 'god', there is only that which is denoted by the name Allah, and **Muhammad (SAW)** is the *Rasul* of this understanding."

The placement of the calligraphy, being on top and above everything else on the page, is a symbolic representation of the predominant importance this understanding holds in the author's life.

The green light, reflecting from the window of the Word of Unity, opens up from the darkness into luminosity to illustrate the light of Allah's *Rasul*. This light is embodied in the book's title through the author's pen and concretized as the color white, to depict the enlightenment the author aims to attain in this field. As the knowledge of Allah's *Rasul* disseminates, those who are able to evaluate this knowledge attain enlightenment, which is represented by the white background of the back cover.

TRANSLATOR'S PREFACE

The Essence of Man is a re-evaluation, or perhaps a *renovation*, of what has for centuries been indisputably accepted as the fundamental teachings of Islam.

Through a compilation of various writings and talks, Ahmed Hulusi takes his readers back to the core and redefines what it means to be a Muslim.

By deconstructing the outer conventional meanings of the many religious or, more specifically, Islamic labels and concepts, the reader is taken to explore the underlying universal meanings of the symbols and metaphors of their faith, and hence the essence of their self.

What is the purpose of religion? What is Sufism? What state of existence lies beyond death? Who or what is referenced by the name 'Allah'? What was the ultimate reality Muhammad (saw) wanted to share with mankind? Why does one have to engage in certain practices and comply with the *sunnah*? How can one escape 'duality' and advance to higher states of consciousness? And, most important of all, what is the essence of all of these 'essential teachings' man has been advised to follow?

As man progresses on his evolutionary journey from his primordial existence towards realizing his inherent vicegerency, it becomes imperative that he give up his attachment to an external heavenly deity and experience the non-local absolute presence of that universal reality instead…

As Hulusi affirms, 'Faith is an *experience*… not a repetition of words.' If one's faith does not enable the experience of this reality, it may be time to reexamine it…

Aliya Atalay
Istanbul 2012

INTRODUCTION

I felt the need to record the discussions that we held throughout this Ramadan, broadcasted on Expo Channel, as a book, in the hope of reaching those who may not have had the chance to view the programs.

Hence, we compiled this book, comprising of not only of these discussions but also writings that I have not previously shared elsewhere.

The main theme of my most recent writings entails the construal of the Quran in light of the hidden meaning of the letter 'B'...

Hadhrat Ali, the pinnacle of *wilayah* (sainthood) says "I am the walking Quran"... in light of the hadith "Man is the twin brother of the Quran"... He also says, "The secret of the Quran is hidden in *al-Fatiha*, the secret of *al-Fatiha* is hidden in the *Basmalah*, and the secret of the *Basmalah* is hidden in the letter B! I am the point beneath that B!"

Leaving aside the last sentence to the judgment of those who experience this reality, since the secret of the Quran is in the letter B, let us reevaluate the Quran from this perspective.

I want to attenuate the following truth:

There are two ways to approach the Quran.

The first pertains to those who are not aware of the secret denoted by the letter B, or who have heard of it but have not discerned its importance.

The second entails the evaluation of those who read the Quran in light of the meaning referenced by the letter B!

Any person who has embraced the religion of Islam inescapably approaches the Quran in either one of these ways!

Those of the former approach have a completely literal and materialistic understanding of religion, and despite their claim "Allah is omnipresent" they think of Allah as a god in the heavens!

When they pray, they stand before that god! They worship Him to attain His pleasure! They take everything in the Quran literally and apply it in form, based on their 5-sense perception. For, this is the function they are created to fulfill!

As for the latter, even though they may not advocate any labels, they accept and believe in the Rasul of Allah (saw) based on the secret of the letter B; and embrace the reality that all things, perceivable and unperceivable, exist and subsist with the Names of Allah. They are the ones who have attained certainty of the meanings denoted by the Names.

This is the common understanding of all saints and friends of Allah. This is the teaching Sufism aims to give, slowly but surely, to its followers…

While those of the former approach 'forcefully impose' their values upon others and claim the right to talk and judge on behalf of their imaginary heavenly god (whom they have named Allah) and announce as 'unbelievers' anyone who does not look or dress like themselves…

Those of the latter understanding approach everyone with love and tolerance and refrain from judging and criticizing others, condemning only the wrongful acts, not their doers. They advise the truth and show patience in times of trouble. As a result, they attain the level of certainty to Allah from a path within their own depths, and because they are able to observe the same reality on every person, they show respect to everyone.

Read the innumerous volumes written by those of the former and latter views. The only difference you will see among them will be those elucidated by the secret of the letter B as opposed to those that haven't.

Everyone will eternally be together with the understanding they identify with today!

Blessed be our understanding!

He who creates everyone upon a specific task and function, so beautifully approbates and facilitates!

Hopefully, we will be of those who reach the secret of the letter B and evaluate the Quran in this light.

AHMED HULUSI
29 October 2005

CONTENTS

1 From The Source To The Future 1
2 Questioning The Religion Of Islam Once Again 3
3 Poisoning The Well 7
4 Unity Versus Multiplicity 11
5 Inquisition 17
6 The Afterlife 21
7 Enjoy The Experience! 25
8 From The Core To The Shell 31
9 The Symbol Of The Name Allah 35
10 Rahman And Rahim 39
11 The Inspired Self (Nafs-i Mulhima) 43
12 Concealed Duality 47
13 Why Did The Holy Man Die Without Faith? 53
14 Where Is Your Intellect? 57
15 Where Is Consciousness Located In The Brain? 61
16 Basmalah 65
17 Why Salat? 67
18 Faith In Muhammad (Saw) 73
19 The Footsteps Of God! 79
20 Reading The Treasure Map 87
21 Misconceptions On The Islamic Way Of Life (Sunnah) 93
22 The Crux 99
23 The Difference Of Muhammad (Saw) 105
24 Out With The Old And In With The New 111
25 Sunnatullah (The Immutable Constants of Allah's System) 117
26 Sunnat-i Rasulullah (The Sunnah of The Rasul of Allah - The Ethics of Allah) ..127

27 Bi-Izni-Hi (With His Permission) 131
28 Inner & Outer Dimensions (Anfus And Afaq) 137
29 Deity-Centric Religion? 141
30 Knowledge – Will – Power 147
31 How Can You Call It A Lie? 151
32 Brain Blockage 159
33 Bi-Rabbihim 165
34 God's Mysterious Night Of Power 171
35 Do Not Be Fooled! 177
36 Shattered To Pieces 183
37 How Would You Like Your Dream House To Be? 195
38 The Coach Builder 201
39 The Function Of The Reviver 209
40 Read Anew 215
41 Farewell 221
42 Selected Verses From The Book Of Allah 233
About The Author 265

1

FROM THE SOURCE TO THE FUTURE

The privileged, are the recipients of tomorrow's call, not yesterday's!

Some are created to address the past, to those who live in the past. This is how they perform their servitude.

Some are created to address the past, to those who live in the present. This is the requirement of their servitude.

We are of neither!

As servants of Allah, we perform our servitude by carrying those that live in the now to tomorrow!

Rasulullah (saw) has disclosed and expounded everything that is valid and viable until Doomsday. From this truth, we have tried to share with you, to the best of our understanding, the things that apply to today and relate to tomorrow.

We have tried to comply with **Hadhrat Ali**'s words:

"Raise your children not according to the days in which you live, but the days in which they will live!"

We have strived for many years, with many explanations, to aid humanity in **transcending the past** and **recognizing the aspects pertaining to the future**.

We have withdrawn to our village and left the field to those who want to drag the present back to the past… perhaps this way **the thinking minds will have the opportunity to evaluate those on the field more comfortably**.

We have relinquished our desire to disclose the many truths that could have been explained.

We show respect to those who find pleasure in consoling themselves with the stories of yesterday and who are closed off to new knowledge… We hope they will be happy in their worlds…

Let it be known, however, if the knowledge disclosed here, which will remain active in our memory, is well evaluated, the accumulations of yesterday's repetitions can be discarded and one may reach **the extensive ocean of the valley of Islam**.

Everything imparted by Muhammad (saw) is immutable and applicable until Doomsday, despite whatever happens in the world.

In order to comprehend the value of this, one must possess knowledge about the viewpoint disclosed in this book.

2

QUESTIONING THE RELIGION OF ISLAM ONCE AGAIN

Sunnatullah, **the system and order** of **Allah**, which was expounded 1,400 years ago, was concealed by the sultanates at the end of **Hadhrat Ali**'s reign. Nevertheless, through Sufism, metaphors, similes and symbolic language, it reached modern times. If it can be re-evaluated in light of all our current scientific knowledge and technological advancements, it can illuminate the whole of humanity with its light (*nur*) once again.

Blessed are those who can do this!

Let me explain with an example:

Imagine you were beamed back 1,000 years to a tribe in Africa or a remote region in the Far East, and were told **"you have to explain the concept of a television and its mechanics to this tribe."** How would you be able to do this, if not with metaphors, similes and symbols? **And how much of today's science and technology are these examples going to relate? How comprehensible is the mechanism of television going to be via these examples you give?** Will you give up and say, **"What more can I say? Use your head and try to comprehend what I am explaining from these examples!"**

Allah's Rasul (saw) saw everything that has and will transpire until Doomsday and tried to relay this to the people through various examples, metaphors and similes.

The Quran also communicates these realities with allegoric and metaphoric language. In fact, **the magnificent Quran** says:

"And We have certainly presented for the people in this Quran from every kind of example – that they might contemplate (remember their forgotten reality)**!"** (Quran 39:27)

Caution!

As I tried to illustrate with the above example…

One can never see the *actual* reality via examples and symbols, but can acquire an understanding of it.

What we need to do is… **Study the contemporary modern sciences and technology, and discern how these realities have been expressed in Muhammad's (saw) language.**

In other words, to understand how the object is disclosed as the abstract!

Muhammad (saw) told Hadhrat Ali:

"O Ali! Everyone is trying to know Allah (attain *yakeen*, certainty) through one path or another. You be of those who pursue the path of reason."

Discerning how the truths pertaining to science and technology were depicted 1,400 years ago as the **system and order of Allah**, who is far from a being a God in heaven, will clear us from the absurd and outdated interpretations portrayed as 'Muslimism' and enable us to see the timeless validity of this system.

This realization will be the savior of **the intelligent ones**! For, **the intelligent**, upon realizing these truths, will understand the importance of re-evaluating **Islam**, and live their lives in favor of their impending eternal abode.

I quote:

"The past has come and gone my friend; now it's time to express new ideas."[1]

---
[1] Mawlana Jalaladdin Rumi

3

POISONING THE WELL

Now that he was older, he struggled to lift a full pail of water all on his own... As he laboringly tried carrying the water back to his tribe, he deliberately overlooked the leaking water from his aged pail, as this lightened his burden... But by the time he reached his tribe, most of the water had leaked out. Surely he couldn't take back an empty pail to his people! So he topped the pail up with some dirty water nearby and presented the water to his tribe as pure spring water from the 'source'.

Only a few, judging from its taste and cloudiness, were able to tell it wasn't pure water. The majority had no idea, as they didn't know what pure water was, they had never gone to the 'source'. Nevertheless, trusting the old man, the people drank the dirty water thinking it pure, and began telling others "this is what pure water looks and tastes like!"

As people age, the brain works slower and less efficiently... The intellect begins to fall short and is unable to fully comprehend certain things...

Especially when the youth asks some of the most obscure questions... One inevitably falters, fabricates and gives absurd answers, like repairs to the main topic. All because the connection to the source is severed; all because one is unaware of the source...

Some, to protect their patronage from prejudice (harm) even assert ideas like:

"The source is holy! Do not disturb the holy source! We are here and ready to help you in every way..."

However, when their answers contradict the recorded knowledge of the source, they begin to cover and modify the information at the source with ludicrous interpretations like:

"Yes, the source says that, but that is not what the source actually means... The source only says that because you will not comprehend it any other way. What it really means to say is this..."

Hence the information given by the source is misinterpreted, distorted and misdirected.

The reason is simple.

When someone isn't a source, and is incapable of understanding the other sources, they attempt to solve something within their own illogical parameters, and when their patchwork solutions do not correspond with the original source knowledge, they distort it and begin to give interpretations to *make it* comply with their own truth!

There is nothing I wrote in 1966 in my first book ***Revelations*** that I feel or think differently about today. What I said 15 years ago and what I say and write today are all the same. The only reason my thoughts were penned, my talks were recorded as audio and video, was to prevent the information I disclose in my talks from becoming distorted over time.

What I said and wrote then is what I say and write now. This is the requirement of the responsibility I feel towards Rasulullah (saw) and the blessings of Allah.

I pen every word in my writings with the consciousness that one day I will face Rasulullah (saw) and give account of everything I shared.

If I have made mistakes, I bear the responsibility.

But nobody has the right to modify and distort my writings or talks to suit their own ideas!

This is why man has been told:

"If your intellect is inadequate, then at least believe!"

Unfortunately, when one lacks both faith and intellect, it results in contamination of the source!

Please… Do not poison the well! Do not contaminate the source!

4

UNITY VERSUS MULTIPLICITY

We live in this world in a system designed and programmed by Allah, completely confined within the limits of our perception capacity, or 'cocoon', yet behave as though we are the sovereigns of the universe! Be that as it may, we are not even aware of the actual dimensions of the universe about which **Muhammad** (saw) once said **"of the seven heavens, each one within the other is like a ring in the desert!"**

Furthermore, we are unaware of the true nature of the religion disclosed by **Allah's Rasul**, the manifestation of the Knowledge of Allah. Ineffectively, we are trying to apply the limited Bedouin understanding from some 1,400 years ago, **amalgamated with all the nonsense interpretations throughout time**, as 'Muslimism', in the 2000s!

A mentality that sees ascension as travelling to space on a horse or a rocket to meet a heavenly God and receive commandments from Him, in fact even *negotiate* with Him, is the mentality with which Allah's religion is being preached and presented to us today, and we are benignly accepting all this as miraculous knowledge! When are we going to forego this primitive tribal understanding disguised as 'Muslimism' and elevate ourselves to the timeless universal truths embodied as the religion of Islam?

Who is going to say **'stop'** to this nonsense?

Is it not time for an 'illuminator' to come and enlighten us to the reality of Islam and save us from this illogical, unintelligent, nonsense understanding of 'Muslimism'?

Those who 'think' have many questions… But there is none to expound the truth of the system **with logical coherency**, purified from all the nonsense of the past!

The ignorant one is he who knows not that he knows not! It is he who is not aware of his own ignorance and inability to comprehend the truth with an integrated rational reasoning.

'Knowledge' has become like a doormat delivered by the 'imitators', reduced beneath people's feet!

Help us, O *Rabb* of the worlds!

Allah's Rasul Muhammad (saw) was a '*hanif*'; he did not worship any idol or deity. He observed through revelation the 'Origin'; the reality and essence (yet beyond even these concepts) of all, and tried to purify the people from idolatry, over 1,400 years ago… He tried to explain to the people that 'there is no God out there' in need of worship! That every individual has the opportunity to reach (not through form and space!) **their own essence and reality, denoted by the name Allah!**

The path to 'ascension' is open to every individual, through the practice of '*salat*'; an inward turn to one's essence.

There is no God or destination that needs to be reached up in the heavens and hence no prayer or worship should be directed out there!

Everything referred to as 'prayer' is for the individual to actualize their own essential reality, through the path designated and eased by '*al-Fatir*'.

The Sufi saints describe the journey of the mystic as **"the completion of the circular path returning to the point at which one begins."**

Those who travel the path of contemplation begin their journey at the point of individuality, and advance level by level towards the reality of things (*ashya*) observing the Oneness from which everything derives its existence. At this level, they are able to identify with insight, that in respect of their reality, the seeming multiplicity is illusory; existence is ONE. Neither their own selves, nor the various dimensions and universes have ever come into existence! This realization marks the semi-circle, it is the state known as '*fanafillah*'. There is more to this, but it need not be shared here.

Those who have completed the second half of the circle do not stay here, as required by their nature, they continue 'observing'.

They observe **the Knowledge attribute** of the One, manifest as **Power (*Qudrah*)** via the attribute of will denoted by the name *Murid*, in order to create the forms of knowledge pertaining to multiplicity. They observe the transformation of abstract angelic forces (Bearers of the Throne) embodying these forms, into the apparent angelic force named 'Spirit', and all the other angelic forces that are generated by them, and the stage-by-stage formation of the universes and everything within the corporeal worlds. They see the depiction of forms of existence through the manifestation of these angelic forces. They observe all of this with the consciousness of who the actual observer is, that is, without their 'selves!'

These intimates of reality (those who have attained the essential truth of things rather than imitating others) **acquire 'certainity' (*yakeen*) to their *Rabb* and see with absolute clarity that everything Allah's Rasul disclosed 1,400 years ago was and is the result of Allah's system, *sunnatullah*!**

Whoever fails to recognize this yet applies it through imitation will still yield some benefit, despite their loss for failing to recognize the truth will be greater than their gain! Whoever refuses to comply with this system will have punished their own self by falling short of the practices known as prayer.

Every dimension of existence has its own set of laws, and these laws are applicable in that dimension no matter what its reality may be!

The fact that the individual's essence derives from **the One**, does not make those laws any less applicable to him! The wood comprised of atoms will burn, but the atoms themselves will not! Only those of equal ignorance will take the statement "my essence is Reality, and the Reality cannot burn in hellfire" of the ignorant imitators serious enough to believe. He who burns today will burn tomorrow! He who experiences suffering today will experience suffering tomorrow! Whoever you are today is who you will be tomorrow! These are crucial truths!

Those who try to stray you from the path advised by **Muhammad** (saw), whatever their reasoning may be, are only attracting you with illusion to their world of apprehension and deception, and its unfavorable consequences!

One can't receive the nutrients of honey by licking its jar! You can own a whole pharmacy, but if don't use medication, you cannot heal your ills!

Power prevails in life! Allah has the attribute of Power, not impotence! At any given instance, either knowledge-based or action-based power prevails against and demolishes impotence!

Allah has created man as the vicegerent of earth and has adorned him with His own names and attributes!

By applying the practices of prayer, you are not ingratiating yourself with some heavenly God, but **tapping into your own potential to manifest it! As such, you will be acquiring new potential with which you can move on to new dimensions and acquaint yourself with the beings there. If you move on to the next dimension without having acquired these qualities through prayer and meditative exercises, you will be like an item of entertainment for the beings there and will have to suffer the consequences.** This is the purpose of prayer!

Allah, the creator of infinite dimensions in universes within universes, does not *need* your prayers. **Know that, whatever you do, is to help you know your origin and essence so you may manifest the potentials with which you have been adorned!**

Do not waste your time waiting around for the savior (*mahdi*) my friend! The reality of the savior is present within your own essence! Allah who inspires the bee[2] also inspires you, by revealing your reality to you through your very essence. It is the inadequacy of your database that prevents you from recognizing this!

Do not let those who have become complacent and stuck in the ways of the past stop you from practicing the teachings of Allah's Rasul Muhamad (saw).

Allah's Rasul, Muhammad Mustapha (saw) is the only and perfect example in understanding and applying the religion of Islam duly and truthfully.

Blessed are those who understand and comprehend his teachings, and who live their lives in accordance with **his practices of the universal system**, and who thereby, attain eternal bliss…

3 October 2002
Raleigh – NC, USA

---

[2] Quran (16:68)

5

INQUISITION

Questions have no end! There is so much to learn yet such limited time! So much has been disclosed as symbols and metaphors in accordance with the societal conditions 1,400 years ago...

Consider the following...

According to one authentic hadith, when a person is buried in their grave, the two angels 'Munkar' and 'Nakir' come to them and ask: **"Who is your *Rabb*? Who is your *Nabi*? What is your Book?"**

You may wonder who these angels are, from where and how they come to the person, whether the form in which they appear is really their original form or whether they assume different forms to different people, and if every person without exception encounters them...

As I explained in my previous writings, the angel concept denotes a phenomenon without physical dimensions or any parameters pertaining to matter; angels do not have height, weight or shape. Hence, their arrival in the grave can obviously not be a locational one! If anything, we can call it a dimension or a state of existence.

Since existence is based on the holographic principle, it is more befitting to think of angels as projections of various

potentials or forces within the human make-up, rather than as external beings. As such, we may perceive angels (our intrinsic qualities), who are said to comprise of the light of knowledge (*nur*) as the forms that become apparent in one's consciousness as a creation of the brain, based on the database and spiritual state of the person. Since all data are uploaded to the spirit and the person begins to live with the spirit body after death, one's database in this world is equally valid and important in the next.

This means, the faculty of inquisition resides internally within each person and will become activated in one's consciousness, once the person is in their grave, to question them in their new state of existence.

This inquisition will be in regards to the three notions mentioned above.

Note that, the person will not be asked, "who is your God?" but "who is your *Rabb*?"

Why is this so?

'Godhead' implies an external God, whereas '*Rububiyyah*' pertains to an inner dimension within the essence of existence.

The answer to this question, based on the conditions of that environment and the state, and experience of the person, should automatically be, 'my *Rabb* is Allah.' In fact, this answer should be founded on the secret of the letter **'B'**.

I repeat, the answers will be the automatic result of one's entire lifetime and lifestyle, *not* the mere utterances of some words, which even a parrot can do!

Almost anyone who experiences death will go through an initial shock, for suddenly, one will have encountered a state of existence they had never anticipated or thought about in the world. At this stage, *every* single person will automatically question their past; they will inquire into the rights and the wrongs they did.

Indeed, everyone who enters their grave and comes face to face with the reality of this new state of existence, will *necessarily* question their life and belief in the world, and evaluate how adequately they have or haven't prepared for life after death and where they did right and where they went wrong... This is the stage where the angels Munkar and Nakir become manifest in them.

Every person, upon entering this new state of life, will automatically and compulsorily question and check themself to see how prepared they are for the conditions of this new place.

There are two possible lifestyles of worldly life.

One either shapes and lives their life based on the true understanding of the One denoted by the name 'Allah,' or fails to recognize this reality and pursues a life in contradiction with the system, in assumption of an external object or a deity-God who is 'beyond'!

Let us know for certain...

If we attempt to decipher the truth of something via the meanings of the names and attributes that are used to denote it, our chances of reaching the actual truth of it is quite low, as this is a very complicated procedure! Words are inadequate in expressing the experience, and as such, reaching the truth via words is almost impossible.

Like when we see a powerful dream and try to explain it to someone but no matter what we say our words always seem to fall short of thoroughly expressing the feeling of the dream.

Similarly, Rasuls and Nabis perceive and experience many things in their consciousness, sometimes even supported with visions, but unfortunately when they have to put their experience into words the expressions are always far from adequate. This is why, when reading such material, one should think about, and try to understand, the experience *denoted* by these words, rather than the words themselves. To think about, and to try to perceive, the "experience" is a much shorter and clearer path to observe.

Indeed, words are very limited and weak in expressing one's feelings and experiences.

If one has lived life in compliance with the reality of Allah, will they have also evaluated the knowledge imparted by the perfection of the Nabis and directed their life according to these?

Why is the question "who is your Nabi?" and not "who is your Rasul?" when 'faith in the Rasul' is mentioned both in the 'Word of Testimony' and in many verses throughout the Quran?

There are two answers to this:

1. **The perfection of *Risalah*** discloses the reality of existence, which pertains to the first question.
2. The conditions that will provide comfort to the person in that state has to do with whether or not they have used the knowledge imparted by the perfection of *Nubuwwah*.

For example, all practices comprising 'prayer' pertain to one's afterlife and have all been determined through the perfection of *Nubuwwah*.

Through these practices the individual is able to produce a certain level of energy and force with which they can resist the unfavorable circumstances awaiting after death.

On the contrary, if the person has not used the knowledge disclosed by the perfection of *Nubuwwah* and has not engaged in the necessary prayers, they will be deprived of the light (*nur*), energy and force that is generated by prayer, and hence subject to severe suffering in the grave! By 'suffering in the grave' what is obviously meant is the natural consequence of inadequately preparing for life after death by failing to acquire the necessary forces required in the grave and life after. In short, not strengthening the spirit body in order to survive in the next realm.

12 December 2002
Raleigh – NC, USA

6

THE AFTERLIFE

One truth should not veil another truth…

The external aspect of our practices should not veil the internal, and the internal experiences should not veil the external practices!

I was at a Friday prayer once, the *hodja* who was giving the sermon was telling everyone they should keep engaging in prayers, even after the month of Ramadan. He gave reference to the verse in the Quran **"Wa'bud rabbaka hatta ya'tiyakal yakeen."** He translated this as "Pray to your *Rabb* until *death* comes"!

Did not the One who revealed **the Quran** know that the word '*mawt*' meant 'death' in Arabic? Why didn't the verse say **"Wa'bud rabbaka hatta ya'tiyakal MAWT"** but instead it used the word '*yakeen*'?

If '*yakeen*' had meant 'death' then wouldn't we have to say '*kulla nafsin dhaikatul yakeen*'!?

If Allah has used the word '*yakeen*' in a verse one cannot change that to '*mawt*' or vice versa! One may ask 'I wonder why this was used here' but one can never cover it with the meaning of another word that Allah has not used, just because they don't understand it!

The verse **"Every soul (consciousness) shall taste death"**[3] must be understood correctly.

Every individual consciousness is going to experience the event through which the body is going to become inoperative and all communications with the world are going to be severed. The individual is going to be fully conscious and aware of what is happening, and they are going to continue their life in the realm of the grave with the same consciousness.

The word *'akhirah'* (afterlife) is the name of the lifetime that commences after the bodily life in the world ends, and life continues throughout other dimensions of existence. In this respect, the process we explained under **'inquisition'** in the previous chapter will also be a conscious experience. There is nothing to interpret here, it is very clear.

The individual who has engaged in prayers in the world will see and experience the benefits of their practices against the creatures in this new abode. And this lifetime will continue as such until the Doomsday of earth.

With Doomsday, the life in the realm of the grave will come to an end, and every spirit, in the form of its last state at the point of death, will gather in the place known as *'mahshar'*.

This is the stage when every individual will assess and see, in detail, their gain and loss, as a result of their worldly life and the activities. This stage will be particularly long and troublesome for mankind.

After this, in attempt to escape the hell besieging the earth, people will begin to follow the Rasuls and Nabis in which they believed on earth. With this journey, the believers will succeed in making the transition to the dimension known as 'heaven', while those deprived of the light (*nur*) of faith will continue their existence in the dimension known as 'hell'.[4]

Prayer and all practices pertaining to prayer observed by the believers in this world will aid their transition to heaven.

---

[3] Quran 21:35
[4] Please refer to *The Mystery of Man* for more information.

Consequently, those who fail to engage in the practices advised by the Rasuls and Nabis will suffer during this transition.

While those who remain in **'hell'** will continue their lives with their spirit bodies, those who succeed to **heaven** will undergo a type of transformation where they will be purified from their **spirit** bodies and commence a **'luminous'** (*nur*) state of existence.

This is a concise summary of the knowledge disclosed to us by **Allah's Rasul**. This is my understanding and belief and, of course, each will be questioned about their own faith. May Allah enable us all to have faith in His Reality and bestow on us a state of *yakeen*.

15 December 2002
Raleigh –NC, USA

7

ENJOY THE EXPERIENCE!

As we know, **the Quran** refers to the event known as **'death'** as an experience which every **'soul'**, i.e. every **'individual human consciousness and spirit'**, will **'taste'**.

But what exactly is meant by the word **'taste'**? With what intention is this word used?

The word **taste** is usually used in reference to nice and pleasurable things. The original Arabic word *'dhaika'* is also used in the same way. Hence, death is actually a pleasurable, taste-filled event for the conscious spirit, who will have become free from the constraints of the physical-biological body and all its limitations!

Every individual will eventually change dimensions through tasting death. **The Quran** uses the phrase **'tasting death'** to imply this transition of dimensions.

Death is an enjoyable, pleasurable experience, for, through death, the person becomes free from all the restrictions of the physical body and begins an unconditioned existence.

The database formed by all the information acquired by the person in their entire lifetime will begin to perceive and evaluate the new dimension to understand it. This new dimension will seem like a bright, luminous and dazzling environment for the person. They may encounter creatures in this new dimension that they were not able to see before, which impose false information to them, such as the nonexistence of a creator, and ideas about creation existing randomly and independently.

At this point, the **faith** of the person in their earthly life will be of paramount importance. If the person's faith in **Allah's Rasul** and his teachings was not wholesomely established during their earthly life, they will be very susceptible to **the delusions imposed by these creatures and to denying all the values pertaining to true faith. They will not have any spiritual values on which they can rely at this point. They will be unable to activate any of their potential forces pertinent to this new realm, and hence they will be helpless and subject to all sorts of torment from the creatures of this new dimension.**

On the other hand, if the individual's **faith in Allah's Rasul** was solidly established in their earthly life, they will know that the values of their faith are also applicable in this dimension, and that, with the aid of Allah, they will overcome these troubles and not be subject to the delusional effects of these creatures.

Of course, this encounter will occur once death is definite. Those who have near death experiences will not have such encounters, as this experience pertains to the period after which the spirit totally leaves the body and the deceased is left alone before their first ascension.

During this transition, those who are greeted by their close ones and religious leaders in whom they believed, will be face to face with **the manifestation of their own databases**. Just like in the dream world!

The spirit of a conscious person, whoever they may be, will initially begin to ascend towards their own essential reality when the connection to their body is completely severed. The quality of **this ascension** will be determined by the level of purity of their consciousness. Of course, this will not be a physical ascension but one that is directed towards their essence and reality, based on the authenticity, accuracy and purification of their data.

If they believed **they were only the physical body and lived their entire life driven by bodily needs and wants**, the data stored in their spirit will necessitate their return to the body such that they feel themself as the physical body once again. Albeit this time, they will find their body inoperative and totally useless. This is when the person will feel that they are in their grave. In the case of those whose bodies may have been injured, cremated or extinguished somehow, they will encounter their own mechanism of inquisition, independent of the body.

Eventually, in one way or another, the person's mechanism of inquisition will become activated. **According to their belief and database**, their faculty of inquisition will take form in their visual field as the two angels *Munkar* and *Nakir*.

Imagine that! You have spent your entire life confined within the material boundaries of your body, and one day you wake up to find yourself in a completely different dimension, in the midst of events and beings of which you had never imagined! Try to imagine and feel **the shock such a person will experience!**

While some will be prepared for this impending transition due to the knowledge and practices they attained and partook on earth, some will encounter all this with no preparation whatsoever.

This change of environment and all the new events encountered by the person will automatically activate the inquisition mechanism within one's consciousness.

Where am I? What will happen to me? Who actually controls this being? Is there a God? Does Allah exist? If so, what is it, where is it, and so on...

All **these questions will be asked as a result of the person's own conscious database, taking form and materializing as the two angels, Munkar and Nakir.**

Though the rest of this process was already explained in the chapter, '**INQUISITION**', I would like to add another important point while we're on the topic.

How will those who **'died before death'** experience this transition?

'**Dying before death**' has three stages:

a. **The Knowledge** of Certainty (*ilm al-yakeen*)

b. **The Eye** of Certainty (*ayn al-yakeen*)

c. **The Reality** of Certainty (*haqq al-yakeen*)

The first **(Knowledge)** denotes the **certainty** one attains via **first hand observation**. This person will be subject to all the different after-death experiences disclosed above, however, their reactions will be very different.

The second **(Eye)** involves the state of certainty where the person sees, perceives and feels the events as though they are actually living it. This person will also go through all the stages described above.

The third **(Reality)** is the state of certainty attained by only a very few individuals. It effectuates when **saints** at the *'**mardiya**'* (the pleasing self) level or certain exceptional individuals, are prone to '*extraordinary experiences*'. In Sufism, this event is known as '*fath*' (self-conquest). A self-conquest that occurs via *extraordinary experiences* involves only two of the seven stages *self-conquest* comprises.

Although these individuals live in this world with their biological bodies, they also possess, through acquisition, **the independence to live beyond the limitations of their bodies**.

Since they would have already overcome the inquisition process at the point of *'fath'* they will not be subject to it again in the grave.

This is signified by the words **'Allah will not make you taste a second death'** uttered to **Rasulullah** (saw) at the point of his transition. That is to say, since you have already gone through and overcome this process through self-conquest *(fath)* you do not have to live again what everyone else has to go through at the point of **tasting death**.

The chapter **'Fath'** in the Quran also designates this truth; though, those who haven't attained the depth of its true meaning evaluated this chapter in relation to the conquest of Makka alone.

Those devoid of this knowledge, think 'second death' refers to some other form of death in the future.[5]

I will be grateful if I have been able to shed some light upon this topic.

14 January 2003
Raleigh – NC, USA

---

[5] More information about this topic can be obtained in ***A Guide to Prayer and Dhikr*** in the chapter titled 'Self-Conquest' (*fath*).

8

FROM THE CORE TO THE SHELL

There is a Sufi saying '**Hu by origin, Hu by descent**'...

Doubtlessly, the origin or essence of a person and their entire existence is important... However, just as the core matters, so does the shell!

The core is important, for if one is not acquainted with their essence, they will look for **an external God, outside themself far out in space**, deviating from the essence of the **'religion'** disclosed by Muhammad (saw).

Religion has two main purposes. One is to **believe in Allah** such that one fully comprehends that there is no external God. This has to do with the essence. The second purpose pertains to the shell or the outer aspect.

The religion of Islam discloses a system, albeit single-minded theologians seem to deny this...

Some theologians and formalist intellectuals who approach religious texts 'literally', and who are devoid of systematic thinking and the universal knowledge disclosed by modern sciences (e.g. quantum physics, the holographic reality, and so on) confine religion to memorization and imitation, still preaching absurd ideas such as a God sitting on a throne in the heavens, who sends down commandments to His postman-prophets on earth via His angels! According to these people, the *jinni* travel some kilometers up to the heavens where they apparently retrieve information from the angels, and then they relay this information to the psychics on earth!

Far beyond being men of knowledge, such people are the representatives of **materialist Muslimism** based on outdated, archaic, primitive ideas from centuries ago. Whatever their title may be, they are fundamentalists devoid of systematic thought capacity.

How primitive to think there is a God in the heavens, with messenger angels under His command, and postman-prophets on earth! How archaic to think those who obey His commands will be let into paradise, while those disobey will be thrown into hellfire as a punishment!

These people have neither any idea about the reality of Allah, nor any understanding of the dimension referenced to as 'angel'. They don't know that the concept of 'prophethood' does not exist in Islam. Instead, Islam asserts '*Risalah*' and '*Nubuwwah*', which actually have very different meanings to their common conception. They don't even know the purpose for which the religion of Islam has been disclosed to humanity!

Having said all this, let us now focus on the 'shell'…

Those who **imitatively** adopt the reality of **unity** disclosed by the **religion of Islam**, without *discerning* the **'system'** on which it relies, always fall into the following misconception:

"Since there is no God out there, and since the One denoted by the name Allah is the 'Essence' known through the attributes of knowledge and power that comprise the essential reality of the entire existence, there is no God I need to worship! Therefore, I should not need to pray, fast, perform pilgrimage, chant names (*dhikr*) or engage in any other form of spiritual practice! Since I am now at this awareness, I do not have to perform any of this!"

This idea is completely and absolutely incorrect! It is such a misleading thought that its cost is unfathomable![6]

---

[6] I have covered this topic in detail in *Know Yourself*

Yes, the essence of man and the essence of the universe are one and the same. However, what distinguishes man from the rest of creation is his *composition*!

Even though, in respect of his molecular make-up, man exists with all of the beings in that dimensions as a single unified being, in terms of his corporeality and consciousness, he lives independent of and separate from the rest of creation, within the parameters defined by the conditions of his body and level of consciousness. In other words, man's existence depends not on the conditions of his atomic and molecular make-up, but the consciousness formed by the conditions of his cellular dimension. Hence, the unity that is present at a lower level of existence does not shape the life on the higher level; every level's quality of life depends on its own set of conditions.

What does this mean? It means, in respect of unity, no matter how much a person recognizes, feels and experiences their essence as the One Reality, ultimately, the person lives their life dependent on the conditions of their bodily life.

Here's an example:

The body is essentially a molecular structure. At a molecular level, one does not feel hunger, thirst or sickness. Nevertheless, one cannot claim they don't need to eat or drink, or take nutrients and medication when feeling run down, just because they are essentially a molecular structure! For, oblivious of one's molecular reality, one's life is conditioned and shaped according to their cellular dimension.

Just like this, no matter how much one comprehends the 'reality' of the universal essence, their life still depends on the state of their body and spirit!

As such, **the religion of Islam recommends the compulsory practices known as 'prayer' not so we worship and deify a God somewhere beyond, but so that we reach the reality of our essence and manifest this infinite potential within our essence through our brain and upload it to our spirit.**

The energy waves generated by one's brain through the prayers for protection form a magnetic shield around the

person! Prayer activates the protective angelic forces within one's essence. Man is not the only species in the universe! Man needs protection! We must understand this!

If you fail to perform these practices, the necessary energy combinations of expansion will not become activated in your brain and thus, the light of knowledge (*nur*) or energy yielded by them will not be uploaded to your spirit. Consequently, when you taste death and leave your physical body, your spirit body will be deprived of the forces you will need in the next dimension. Since at this point, you will not have the means to produce this force, due to not having the physical brain, you will forever feel the agony and pain of this deprivation. You will have thrown yourself into the hellfire with your own hands.

Allah need never punish His servants. Everybody will live the consequences of their own doings.

We must comprehend this reality well...[7]

27 January 2003
Raleigh – NC, USA

---

[7] More information on this topic can be obtained in *Allah, The Voice of the System, Know Yourself* and *A Guide to Prayer and Dhikr*.

9

THE SYMBOL OF THE NAME ALLAH

As known, the *Basmalah*, 'In the Name of Allah…' denotes that **'Allah'** is a name.

A 'name' is a sign that points to the one who is 'named'.

When I say 'the One denoted by the name Allah' I try to introduce a different perspective to the topic. This time, I want to take yet another perspective and focus on the original Arabic symbol of the word 'Allah'.

Anyone familiar with the Sufi way will know that existence comprises four worlds: the World of the Absolute Essence, the World of Attributes, the World of Names, and the World of Acts. The return to one's essence and the acquisition of self-knowledge requires experiencing these worlds.

As known, the word **'Allah'** is written in Arabic with the letter *aleph* (ا), which stands alone and independent from the other letters, followed by two *lām*s (ل) and a *he* (ه) in the shape of a circle (or a square in the case of Kufi calligraphy) attached to the second *lām*. There is also an invisible *aleph* between the second *lām* and *he*, which can't be seen but is read to give the sound **'a'**.

Let's have a look at the meanings these letters symbolize... Though, of course, this evaluation is based on the discovery of the enlightened ones (*ahlul kashf*) and are not binding, I want to share them anyway as it may aid in some of our assessments...

The first **aleph** signifies the **Ahad** quality of Allah and points to **His Absolute Essence**. The Absolute Essence is independent from all things and cannot be conditioned by any attributes, ideas or thoughts. It is such a state of 'nothingness' that none can ponder on or contemplate it; it cannot be understood or explained. Thus, the letter **aleph**, which is essentially an extension of a point, represents absolute independence.

The first **lām** following the **aleph** signifies the world of attributes. Everything in existence derives its life, consciousness and power from the qualities of this dimension. All of the worlds are expressions of the names, which originate from the qualities of the world of attributes. As such, the first **lām** is connected to the second **lām**.

The second **lām** is also connected to the first **lām** as its existence is derived from and is sustained by the qualities of the world of attributes. All the qualities of the names, present within the dimension of names, obtain their life from the world of attributes. Hence, the second **lām** seems like a repetition of the first **lām** (because it derives its existence from the first *lām*), but in terms of its implications, it denotes a completely different dimension of manifestations.

The letter **he** is connected to the second **lām** and drawn either as a circle or, in the case of Kufi calligraphy, a square. It signifies the constant manifestations of the world of names and attributes, the flow of qualities without beginning or end, the constant transformation of the world of acts, that is, the world of activities, or everything that transpires and is perceived within the multiple universes!

The *shaddah* or, 'sign of emphasis' on top of the **he** (which is used to *double* the consonant) designates the dichotomy between the manifest and the hidden aspects of the world of acts, in view of the perceiver.

The *he* is connected to the second *lām* because the world of acts does not exist independent from the worlds of acts and attributes. It is in fact sustained with the manifestations of the qualities pertaining to the world of acts and the world of attributes.

There is also, between the letters *he* and the second *lām*, a hidden *aleph*, whose existence is acknowledged only when read. This symbolizes the dependence of the world of acts on the will and wish of the Absolute Essence, as it draws its life and existence from His knowledge, attributes and names.

The insightful and enlightened ones will recognize the truth in this construal more comprehensively and truly evaluate and appreciate the name '**Allah**' in terms of what it actually symbolizes.

I hope this knowledge, authenticated via insight, will enable us to understand and appreciate the subtlety in the word **'Allah'** and allow us to use it more appropriately in the future.

29 January 2003
Raleigh – NC, USA

10

RAHMAN and RAHIM

We usually just say the *Basmalah* without much thought... Then we recite the Fatiha for our dead! Whereas, the Rasul of Allah has warned us **"*Salat*, without the Fatiha, cannot be!"**

As we know, the *Basmalah* is '*Bismillah-arRahman-arRahim*'. It is both the first verse of the Quran, and, based on a joint understanding, the first verse of the opening chapter, al-Fatiha.

Some say the *Basmalah* cannot be considered as the first verse of **al-Fatiha** because the first verse of al-Fatiha is **"*Alhamdu lillahi Rabbil alameen*"** (i.e. "*Hamd* **belongs to Allah, the** *Rabb* **of the worlds**"). This topic has been discussed in detail in the late Elmalili Hamdi's interpretation of the Quran.

I want to approach the topic from a different angle here and try to discern the reason for the repetition. That is, if the *Basmalah* is the first verse of **al-Fatiha** then why is '*Rahman-arRahim*' repeated again in the third verse?

"*Bismillah-arRahman-arRahim*

Al hamdu lillahi Rabbil alameen

Ar Rahman ar-Rahim..."

I want to draw your attention to the mystery of the letter 'B' in the beginning of the **Basmalah**. I had expounded this mystery in **Muhammad's Allah** by referencing the late Hamdi Yazir's interpretation[8] in regards to the letter **B**:

*Acclaimed interpreters claim that the letter B here denotes either 'specificity' or 'association' or else 'to seek help'... Based on this construal, the translation of the Basmalah (which begins with the letter B) should be: 'For, or **on behalf** of Allah, who is Rahman and Rahim' which denotes contingency. This is an admission of 'vicegerency'. To begin an activity with the words 'ON behalf of Him' means 'I am engaging in this activity in relation to, as a vicegerent to, as the representative of, and as the agent of Him, therefore this activity is not mine or someone else's but only His'. This is the state of annihilation in Allah (fana fi-Allah) pertaining to the concept of Unity of Existence.*

In light of this knowledge, we may say that, based on the reality denoted by the letter 'B', the **Rahman** and **Rahim** attributes of Allah emerge from the **self**. As such, the person can reach the bounties of *Rahman* and *Rahim*, both manifest and hidden, through his own essence.[9]

The next verse points to the apparent aspect of things, that is, the facet of the universe that the individual is capable of perceiving. In other words, all perceivable things in all dimensions of existence sustain their existence with the *Rahman* and *Rahim* qualities present in the Name-composition of their essence (*Rububiyyah*).

While the first verse designates *Uluhiyyah* as a derivation of one's essence, the second and third verses indicate that the perfection of ***Uluhiyyah***, which generates from the point of ***Rububiyyah*** within the essence of every individual in the universe, is composed of the ***Rahman*** and ***Rahim*** qualities.

This means, the first verse signifies the mystery of **'knowing one's self'** and the second verse denotes the mystery of **'knowing the reality of *things (ashya)*'**.

---

[8] Page 42-43 Vol 1 of 9, *Hak Dini Kur'an Dili*, by Elmalili Hamdi Yazir
[9] For more information on the topics of Rahman and Rahim please refer to *The Essential Principals of Islam*

Having said all of this, let us now think about who and what exactly we are referring to when reciting the following during bowing and prostration in *salat*:

"Subhana Rabbi al-Azim!"

"Subhana Rabbi al-A'la!"

What does it mean for **my** *Rabb* **to be** *Subhan***,** *Azim* **and** *A'la*?

What is the intention behind repeating these words? What are we supposed to grasp and feel while making this invocation?

May Allah allow and facilitate its comprehension for us…

28 February 2003
Raleigh –NC, USA

11

THE INSPIRED SELF
(NAFS-I MULHIMA)

There are seven stations of the self...

Ammarah (inciting), *lawwama* (self-accusing), *mulhima* (inspired), *mutmainna* (peaceful), *radhiya* (pleased), *mardhiya* (pleasing) and *safiya* (pure)![10]

The word 'self' (*nafs*) refers to the individual consciousness.

Based on its database, when the individual consciousness is first formed, it assumes the wants of the body as its own, and as such, bases its existence on corporeality and the body. This phase is referred to as the inciting self (*nafs-i ammarah*).

When the self, which confines itself to its body, realizes that life will not end with the death of the body, that it will somehow continue, and it will have to face the consequences of its actions in this world in the next realm of existence, the remorse it feels for its mistakes that endanger its future is known as accusation (*lawm*), and hence defined as the self-accusing self (*nafs-i lawwama*).

In both cases the self, or individual consciousness, is based around and related to the body. That is, all that transpired relates to

---

[10] More information on this topic can be found in *Know Yourself*

the 'earth' (*ardh*)! The individual consciousness is yet unaware of its heaven (*sama*)!

When the individual consciousness realizes that it is not the body but the reflector and manifestation of universal oneness it is called the inspired self (*nafs-i mulhima*) as this realization is through internal inspiration.

At this level the individual consciousness begins to refine itself of the bodily notion. At times it will feel like the body, and at times, as something else... Though, at this stage, it will not be able to define the nature of its 'other than the body' self, as this is not a reality that one can intellectualize with knowledge.

This level of individual consciousness is probably the most difficult. It will fall in and out of many contradictions. At times it will see itself as the servant and at times it will see itself as the Reality, and based on these it will experience different results!

Only a very few people are able to overcome this phase.

One who sees themselves as the Reality at this stage, may not even deign to consider sainthood (!) They may even neglect and omit all religious practices and indulge in bodily life.

For the people of authenticity, the act of **READING** commences here. They begin to **READ THE SYSTEM** called *sunnatullah*, and at this level of consciousness, they discern the reality of what the Rasul of Allah brought and why, they begin to experience this reality at the level of certainty (*haqq al-yakeen*).

Here, he will have freed from all concepts of duality (*hanif*)! Here he will truly believe in **the One denoted by the name Allah**...

Here he will become purified through suffering (*kashf-i zulmani*) and attain enlightened discovery (*kashf-i nurani*).

Here he will discern the secrets of the **Quran** valid until Doomsday ...

A person at this level is deemed enlightened and called an '*arif*'. However, they have not yet attained sainthood.

The ones who the masses, or those who imitate rather than contemplate, call 'saint' and appropriate titles such as 'gaws', 'qutub' etc. comprise this level of consciousness. Sometimes even they begin to believe they are deserving of these titles, because of the unveiling they experience. Whereas, at this stage, all of their insight and knowledge are like mere droplets from the fountain of sainthood.

The station of **sainthood** is yet oceans away…!

28 March 2003
Raleigh – NC, USA

12

CONCEALED DUALITY

Let us remember and be mindful of the following:
1. Allah will definitely not forgive duality. Everything else is open to forgiveness by Him, if He wishes to do so…
2. **Allah disfavors those who overstep and exceed their place**.
3. **Allah disfavors the ungrateful**.

Keeping these in mind, let's now try to discern this topic…

The Quran does not categorize **'duality'**. As far as the Quran is concerned, **duality** is **duality**, whether concealed or apparent. However, there are two forms of duality connected to the two aspects of faith, which are:
1. Faith in Allah
2. Faith in Allah with the secret of the letter **'B'**!

The two aspects of duality are:
1. Apparent duality; deifying an external object or one's body.
2. Hidden or concealed duality; denying the One denoted by the name **'Allah'** by denying the secret of the letter **'B'**.

As noted above, **Allah does not favor the ungrateful**. We usually interpret the act of ungratefulness as not knowing the value, not being thankful and displaying unappreciative behavior toward a good that is done or given by someone to us.

Whereas the verdict **'Allah does not favor the ungrateful ones'** denotes the deeper reality that Allah wants His servants to discover and appraise the names and attributes endowed within their essence.

As such, **the ungrateful ones** are those who do not live by the names and attributes comprising the reality of their consciousness, and who instead confine their existence to the physical body and its physical stimuli and desires, living their life as if the sole purpose of their existence is to satisfy their bodily wants.

As for the second statement, **'Allah does not favor those who overstep and exceed their place'**, we usually understand this as, 'If someone transgresses the boundaries imposed upon them it means they are exceeding their place'. **Whereas, the very purpose of man's creation is what defines his boundaries!**

Man (not *humanoid*) has been created as the **vicegerent** of earth. The only way he can actualize this and attain the level of 'the most dignified of all creation' is if he becomes worthy of the principle of **'vicegerency'**. This will only be possible if he recognizes and believes in **his conscious-self beyond his body-self**, know with certainty that the association with his body is temporary and will be eternally abandoned at some point, and align his life with the universal reality disclosed by the **Rasul of Allah**!

Otherwise, as a result of deifying and serving his body, he will be of the transgressors, **disfavored by Allah**. He will be reduced to the state of Iblis, who was expelled from the presence of Allah. **All of the doors of spirituality will be closed to him**. Thus, for the sake of a few years of bodily temptations he will forever suffer the misery of falling separate from Allah.

He who does not learn from yesterday's mistakes will not be able to evaluate today and will be damned to repeat the same mistakes tomorrow!

This directs us to the topic of **duality** (*shirq*)...

The **Quran** does not differentiate between types of duality. However, in order to ease its understanding it has been categorized as two types. External or apparent *duality* and internal or concealed *duality*; all of these terms have been used to refer to the duality formed in one's individual consciousness.

The **Rasul of Allah** (saw) says: "After me, my people will not openly engage in external duality, **what I fear on behalf of them is the hidden type of duality**." That is, they will not be aware that their deeds will have implications of concealed duality.

Eventually, it does not matter what type, duality is duality, and is **not subject to forgiveness**.

When Allah's Rasul says "I fear for my people" it is in terms of duality being an **unforgivable** act, regardless of its type.

What does this mean in respect of *sunnatullah*?

Since there is no God what does it mean for duality not being subject to forgiveness? *Who* will not forgive duality? What are the reasons and consequences of this?

***Shirq* is the name given to the act of deifying and serving things other than the One denoted as Allah. This deity may be an external or an internal one (self).**

Whereas the One denoted by Allah has created the individual to serve only Him!

But what does it mean to serve only Allah?

When the person recognizes and activates the qualities of the Names comprising their essence within their consciousness, that is, when they adorn themselves with the morals of Allah, or, express their potential divine qualities as much as their brain allows, they are serving Allah. This is the purpose! As for the 'means', it includes the various practices known as 'prayer', diets that need to be done at certain times, and acquiring the kind of knowledge to enable conviction and certainty in this path.

What prevents man from adhering to these practices is his illusion of corporeality and mistaking his bodily desires as the desires of his consciousness! This illusion is the person's devil! A humanoid is one who is a servant to this illusion! For such a person only bodily pleasures, relationships, and a lifestyle based on corporeality is real. Hence, these people have been defined as 'dualists' (people of *shirq*). Once a person is caught up by such ideas, it is very difficult for them to escape! Thus, duality (*shirq*) is said to be 'unclean' (*najis*)!

"**Verily the dualists** (who claim the existence of their ego-identities alongside the Absolute Oneness) **are contaminated**..." Quran (9:28)

On the other hand, the Quran refers to the purified (*tahir*) as:

"**...None but the purified** (from the dirt of *shirq* – duality – animalistic nature) **can touch it** (i.e. become enlightened with the Knowledge of the Absolute Reality)." (Quran 56:79)

For, as long as one is in a state of duality, they will not be able to clearly discern the truth.

If the individual consciousness confines itself to the physical body and lives in pursuit of bodily pleasures at the expense of causing harm to others, then the ritualistic practices they may observe in the name of prayer will only be their way of deluding themself to ease their conscience.

The message is definite:

Allah will not accept any of the deeds of the dualist. The dualist does injustice only to their self.

As for dualism being an **unforgivable** act...

A person whose life is driven by bodily stimulations rather than the essence of their consciousness, that is, the One denoted by the name Allah, squanders all their energy and thoughts on things they will indefinitely leave behind in this world. Consequently, their spirit will only be loaded with worldly data that will be totally useless in the afterlife. As they will not encounter the people and events of this world in the next, the data pertinent to this world will be rendered invalid in the next plane of existence.

Man must acquire and use the primary forces of the 'System' in order to survive in future dimensions!

If he allows his worldly conditionings, values and emotions to restrict himself to his body and bodily amusement then he will be automatically deprived of the qualities mentioned above.

Therefore, if we are ungrateful to the knowledge disclosed to us by the **Rasul of Allah, transgressing our boundaries**, we will partake in activities inducing corporeality, and thus, **in the dimension where each will face the consequences of their own doings**, we will live **the results of duality** as **injustice to our selves**! For, in the mechanics of the System known as *sunnatullah* there is neither place nor forgiveness for duality.

Allah does not favor the transgressors!

Allah does not favor the ungrateful!

Those who engage in duality and are unjust to themselves for the pleasure of a few fleeting things, will suffer eternal misery and expulsion!

Whether concealed or apparent, duality remains just that: duality!

19 June 2003
Raleigh – NC, USA

13

WHY DID THE HOLY MAN DIE WITHOUT FAITH?

We look at the way some people speak and act and say '**he's like a saint!**' Then it turns out he passed to the next plane of existence **void of faith**. This fascinates us. How can a man whose knowledge and behavior convinces us of its saint-like qualities, die as an unbeliever?

When I pondered this question I observed the following:

The **Rasul of Allah** (saw) says: **"The state in which one lives is the state in which he will die, be resurrected and transit from the dimension of the grave to the place of gathering (*mahshar*)."**

There are two types of memory in the brain: short-term memory and **long-term memory**. The **short-term memory** is used for daily data and momentary evaluations. This sometimes lasts a couple of hours, and sometimes extends until the end of the day. The part of consciousness operating here at times transfers and stores some of this data in the long-term memory, and at times deletes it, just like the RAM and the hard disk.

While we store all the information, conditionings and value judgments we obtain from the past and through genetic inheritance in our long-term memory, the consciousness in our short-term memory (like RAM memory) evaluates the present moment, based on the stimuli the brain receives from the body through hormones and emotions.

As needed, the short-term memory accesses the data in the long-term memory.

According to my understanding, this is critical to understanding our topic. For, **while the intellect goes about its business using the short-term memory, regardless of the kind of information stored in the long-term memory, during decision-making the intellect will always be subject to the influence of bodily impulse and emotions.**

Bodily stimuli and emotions, primarily triggered by hormones, pertain to the biochemical makeup of the body as a whole.

Those who are familiar with the subject will already know that **too much or too little of one's hormone production** can cause significant changes and **imbalances to a person's psychology**. As such, **bodily stimuli, astrological influences, environmental conditionings and incorrect information** play profound roles in the evaluation of data in one's short-term memory. Oblivious of correct or incorrect data that may be stored in the long-term memory; these can instigate contrary behavior and result in incorrect evaluation and applications.

My personal understanding is that an **unhealthy liver** leads to a sequence of imbalances in one's metabolic and biochemical makeup, which is then **reflected to the brain**, causing the intellect to make incorrect judgments and interpretations in the short-term memory. **As such, anything that may be harmful to the liver should be avoided in order to maintain a healthy thought system and a healthy brain.**

If the individual **consciousness** denoted by the word *'nafs'*, i.e. self (not the body), **can align its existence according to the truthful data in the long-term memory**, despite the bombardment of astrological influences, bodily stimuli and emotions, its life will flourish both in this world and the next. This can only happen **if they 'tame their *nafs* (self)' by purifying themself with the practices of Sufism and the knowledge of Islam**. On the contrary, they will have a troublesome time not only in this world but also in the next.

Originally, *salat* was offered as 40 times a day, and then eventually reduced to five. Why five?

The Rasul of Allah, Muhammad Mustapha (saw), who had the clearest comprehension and understanding of the Quran, always prayed five times a day; he and his followers performed *salat* throughout their whole lives. The implication of this is that *salat* **is something that is lived and experienced** rather than performed.

Let us be mindful of the warning "**woe to those who are unaware** of the *salat* they perform". That is, as the saying goes, "*Salat* **cannot be done without the Fatiha**"; the person must ponder on and experience the meaning of the verses they recite during *salat*. This contemplation is what allows them to enter the essence of *salat*. Through this meditative contemplation the person realizes their body is only a temporary means of transport for them, and that they are a '**vicegerent' endowed with 'divine' potentials** that need to be discovered and actualized from their dormant potential state before making the transition to the afterlife.

This realization and remembrance shapes the intellectual activity in the short-term memory and drives one's life in the direction of this newly obtained data, for a particular period of time. During waking hours, this period is sectioned into five. As such, depending on the person's short-term memory performance, they spend their lifetime in 'faith', until the next time!

In fact, *salat* is not limited to a period of time, rather every period has its own *salat*.

One may read religious teachings word by word, memorize the Sufi way and store it in long-term memory such that it can be retrieved whenever it is needed, just like a computer. Thereby, they may appear to be 'saint-like', yet in reality be no more than a philosopher!

If, during their evaluation of the present moment, their consciousness does not prevent them from becoming captivated by their bodily impulses, or if their emotions cause them to display contrary behavior to their logic, intellect and the 'knowledge of faith' stored in their long-term memory, this will lead them to become blinded and act oblivious to the realities of faith. For such a **'faithless' person, 'tasting' death will not even be an option**! They will die and be resurrected as an 'unbeliever.'

Therefore, yielding to physical impulses and emotions and behaving adversely to the intellect is a clear implication that one does not have faith in having an immaterial existence created to live eternally beyond death. Such a person's experience of death will concur with the 'faithless' state in their short-term memory, regardless of how many people feel drawn to their knowledge and speech, and attribute **saint-like behavior** to them.

This is a very comprehensive topic; I only shared the general outline of my understanding of it. Further contemplation will most assuredly assist in discovering much more…

Do we ever ponder how much high cholesterol and hormonal imbalances can affect our brain performance and psychology?

Do we think about how metabolic imbalance caused by consuming things that are harmful to our liver, disrupts our brain's biochemical energy, resulting in psychological disorder?

As I said, this is a very elaborate topic. Man's current level of knowledge in this area is like performing brain surgery with an axe!

Abstaining from things that are detrimental to our brain, liver and hormonal balance will perhaps bring about unimagined fortune to us in the hereafter…

Let us now ponder on this…

29 June 2003
Raleigh – NC, USA

14

WHERE IS YOUR INTELLECT?

We say things like **"come to your senses!"** or **"what were you thinking?"** yet hardly ponder on where exactly our **'intellect'** or **'faculty of reason'** really is…

Well, here is a story:

Almighty God created the intellect, adorned it with supreme qualities and then placed it on top of the brain. The intellect looked around itself, but was not able to see anything. It thought "Is it dark in here or am I blind?"… Not being able to find a solution to the problem, the intellect asked God: "Dear God, you created me in perfect form, yet I think I am blind! You designed me to be dynamic, active, vivacious and adaptable, yet I am unable to see anything ahead of me, behind me or around me! I can't even see where I am! All I can do is evaluate the data that comes to me and redirect it according to its purpose as best I can…"

God replied: "I have created you so perfectly that it is unnecessary for you to have eyes. In order for you to perform your function, it is better that you are blind. I have placed you in this location; everything you need is at your disposal. All you have to do is evaluate the incoming data. You are in the center of the universe! If you evaluate the incoming data well, you will become the sultan of where you are. Remember, I have also provided for you, in the same location, the power of faith, in case you encounter a dilemma or find yourself in some sort of predicament..."

The intellect was pleased with this answer and began to perform its task accordingly...

However, when mankind increased in number, and the intellect in every person started encountering different data, the overwhelming confusion, the misleading data and perhaps a little hormonal stimulus, tripped the intellect over, causing it to flow into the bloodstream! Before it knew, it was in another organ! But because it was blind, it was unable to recognize this new place (organ) and thought it was back in its original location. Nevertheless, it continued to evaluate the incoming data from this new organ in a most perfect fashion, carrying out its function effectively!

This new location is the stomach for some people, the reproductive organs for others... It is the feet for some, and the heart for others!

Hence, some people live only to eat and consume, some only to engage in sexual activity, some commit their entire lives to sports, and others live their lives driven by emotions alone, constantly feeling regret and remorse...

Indeed, when the intellect, the faculty of reason falls from its sacred throne, the brain, people say "come to your senses!" But alas! How can one possibly do so, when one's intellect has settled in some other organ and its brain has become this new organ?

...

The solution?

...

FAITH!

...

Either the power of faith will manifest itself and bring back the intellect to its throne, or if unable to persuade it, it will cease its connection with the intellect altogether! In this case, the intellect will pursue its life without faith and change dimensions without the power of faith!

And from a distance, the watchers will say:
"Another one has passed without faith…"

29 July 2003
Raleigh – NC, USA

15

WHERE IS CONSCIOUSNESS LOCATED IN THE BRAIN?

We have become so accustomed to living our lives without contemplating and questioning that we take solace in relating the things we can see to 'matter' and the things we can't see to magic! Some call this magic 'mother nature' and some call it 'God'! It is as though we unwisely insist on not seeing the magnificent mechanism of the body, the cause-and-effect relation and the perfection of the **brain**, which is the most elevated mechanism of the **One denoted by the name 'Allah'**!

So-called scholars and their heralds who have no idea about the role of genes in the creation and life of man and its place and function in the brain, console the masses with nonsense ideas such as man being some sort of a hocus-pocus creation of God and all man has to do is deify and worship this God!

We are afraid of thinking, questioning and knowing ourselves!

Narrators of Quranic verses and hadith have no idea about the modern scientific developments, and most scientists are unaware of the pure knowledge disclosed by 'religion'. Many people pass through this world living in their own imaginary worlds.

In fact, the System and Order implied by the word **'religion'**, created by **the One denoted as 'Allah',** can only be truly appraised and evaluated by those who can use their brain, which is what drives scientific developments. As such, **the most realistic approach entails deciphering the brain's mechanism to understand how this influences our thoughts and behavior.**

Of course, I have nothing to say to those who claim:

"I am happy enough with praying five times a day and fasting in Ramadan. I want no further involvement in anything else". By all means, they too will face the consequences of their deeds.

I am addressing those who claim to be researchers and intellectuals, who accept and deny science as they wish, and when fed up with thinking, resort to God's magic wand.

Abdulkarim al-Jili, in his *Perfect Man* says: **"This world is the world of wisdom; the afterlife is the world of power"**.

Including **Muhyiddin ibn al-Arabi**, all Sufis assert that everything in this world transpires through causes. However, due to our lack of knowledge, we do not always apprehend them. It is based on this reason that **Ibn Arabi** claims **everything in this world, the intermediary dimension (*barzakh*), the place of gathering (*mahshar*), and heaven and hell, are all under the influence of star signs.** Even though, the kinds of waves astrological influences are carried through still remains unknown.

At this point, I would like to share a very important note regarding the brain.

In the chapter titled **"Were spirits created in pre-eternity?"** in my book *Islam* I talked about how **our spirits are formed in the mother's womb rather than being instilled into our bodies from an outside source. Thus, the word 'spirit' in religious terminology, the afterlife body, is created by the nucleus of the brain in the mother's womb.**

Individual consciousness and memory, products of the brain, are stored in the spirit, such that, when the spirit's connection to the body is severed, the spirit continues to live with the same consciousness. My understanding of 'the book that we are going to read at the place of gathering (*mahshar*)' is this: where not even a comma of your life will be omitted.

This is one of the biggest miracles of the One denoted by the name Allah. How does the energy we obtain from the food we eat reach our brain in the form of certain waves? This is a point worth pondering for anyone with an intellect.

Does the brain produce waves? Every scientist now confirms the existence of various waves produced by the brain. What is unknown are the specific functions they serve. There is still some ambiguity in this area. Due to the lack of technical facilities, the entire wave spectrum produced by the brain is still largely unknown.

In 1985, when I wrote about how the human spirit does not enter the body from the outside, and the brain produces it, nobody had even addressed this topic. Now, in 2002, Professor Johnjoe McFadden from the School of Biomedical and Life Sciences at the University of Surrey in the UK is claiming our conscious mind could be an electromagnetic field:

What Professor McFadden realized was that every time a nerve fires, the electrical activity sends a signal to the brain's electromagnetic (em) field. But unlike solitary nerve signals, information that reaches the brain's em field is automatically bound together with all the other signals in the brain. The brain's em field does the binding that is characteristic of consciousness.

What Professor McFadden and, independently, the New Zealand-based neurobiologist Sue Pockett, have proposed is that ***the brain's em field is consciousness.***

The brain's electromagnetic field is not just an information sink; it can influence our actions, pushing some neurons towards firing and others away from firing. This influence, Professor McFadden proposes, is the physical manifestation of our conscious will.

"The theory solves many previously intractable problems of consciousness and could have profound implications for our concepts of mind, free will, spirituality, the design of artificial intelligence, and even life and death," he said.

Most people consider "*mind*" to be all the conscious things that we are aware of. But much, if not most, mental activity goes on without awareness. Actions such as walking, changing gear in your car or pedaling a bicycle can become as automatic as breathing.

The biggest puzzle in neuroscience is how the brain activity that we're aware of (*consciousness*) *differs from the brain activity driving all of those unconscious actions.*

When we see an object, signals from our retina travel along nerves as waves of electrically charged ions. When they reach the nerve terminus, the signal jumps to the next nerve via chemical neurotransmitters. The receiving nerve decides whether or not it will fire, based on the number of firing votes it receives from its upstream nerves.

In this way, electrical signals are processed in our brain before being transmitted to our body. But where, in all this movement of ions and chemicals, is consciousness? Scientists can find no region or structure in the brain that specializes in conscious thinking. Consciousness remains a mystery.

"*Consciousness is what makes us 'human,'*" Professor McFadden said. "*Language, creativity, emotions, spirituality, logical deduction, mental arithmetic, our sense of fairness, truth, ethics, are all inconceivable without consciousness.*" But what's it made of?[11]

The electromagnetic field created by brain waves is the pivotal point of this article...

Whether or not this electromagnetic field is the phenomenon we have come to call '**spirit**', it is an undeniable fact that the brain produces waves, which are now being considered as 'consciousness'.

One day, science will also discover the afterlife body, the spirit, as comprising certain brainwaves of energy that differ from our physical body.

Albeit, I probably won't be here to see it...

23 October 2003
Raleigh – NC, USA

---

[11] http://www.unisci.com/stories/20022/0516026.htm

16

BASMALAH

Previously, I had written about the *Basmalah*, both in the section about al-Fatiha in *The Essential Principals of Islam* and in earlier chapters in this book. This time, I would like to expound another aspect of it...

In congregational prayer, the *Basmalah* is not recited by the *Imam*, even though it is the first verse of the chapter al-Fatiha. The *Imam* always begins reciting from the verse "*Alhamdu lillahi Rabbil alameen.*" Why does the *Imam* not recite the *Basmalah* first? I presume this is something most people don't really think about... Indeed, the general practice entails the *Imam* reciting from the second verse of chapter al-Fatiha, skipping the first verse, the *Basmalah*, whereby the people in the congregation each recite the *Basmalah* to themselves in order to **complete (!)** the recitation!

Let us first clarify an age-old discussion: Some say the chapter al-Fatiha comprises seven verses and its first verse is the *Basmalah*. Some say the first verse of **al-Fatiha** is not the ***Basmalah,*** it is "***Alhamdu lillahi Rabbil alameen***" and that the *Basmalah* at the beginning is placed there to highlight the productiveness of the prayer.

Those with an in-depth and comprehensive understanding of the topic all agree that the *Basmalah* is indeed the first verse of the chapter al-Fatiha. This is my understanding also.

In this case, one questions, why after reciting "*Rahman-ar-Rahim*" in the *Basmalah*, the verse after "*Alhamdu lillahi Rabbil alameen*" repeats "*Rahman-ar-Rahim*"?

That is,

The first verse: ***"Bismillah-ar-Rahman-ar-Rahim"***

The second verse: ***"Alhamdu lillahi Rabbil alameen"***

The third verse: ***"Ar-Rahman-ar-Rahim."***

As I had mentioned in a previous article about *Rahman* and *Rahim*, the subtle reality here is that **the person engaged in *salat*, must experience the meaning of the *Basmalah*, in respect of the secret denoted by the letter 'B', if they want their *salat* to become an ascension (*miraj*)!**

As such, it is insufficient for the *Imam* to recite the *Basmalah* on behalf of the congregation. The *Basmalah* must be recited and experienced by the person personally, so they *can* commence their prayer with that appreciation.

In other words, the *Imam* cannot recite the *Basmalah* on behalf of the congregation. For ascension (*miraj*) to take place, **every individual must experience the reality of the *Basmalah* in person!**

Blessed are those who can experience the reality of the *Basmalah* at least once every day!

Wassalam...

10 April 2004
Raleigh – NC, USA

17

WHY SALAT?

We have been addressed as **'humans'**…

What exactly is a **human** though? To what does the word 'human' actually refer?

I covered this topic in detail in *Know Yourself* and *Purification of Consciousness* so I will omit the detail here…

Briefly, however, I would like to share what I believe *salat* is, why it has been offered to man, and **why it is compulsory**…

Recent technological advancements have spawned some profoundly incredible robots. Also recently, the movies '**Artificial Intelligence**' and '**I, Robot**' were screened depicting robots with emotions…

If we were to upload the recitation of the Quran to a robot, and program it to perform the actions of the *salat* at specific times, no doubt it will be able to perform the *salat*, reciting the whole of the Quran, with exceptional performance and remarkable accuracy. In fact, we can even program it to shed a few tears here and there!

So, what distinguishes us from a robot? Do we know our difference?

Man's quality of distinction is his ability to contemplate on what he recites, to comprehend and experience its meaning and to continue its application after *salat*!

"**So woe to those who pray** (due to tradition), **who are heedless** (cocooned) **of** (the experience of the meaning of) **their** *salat* (which is an ascension [*miraj*] to their innermost essential reality; their *Rabb*)"[12]

So what is the experiential reality of *salat*?

I am not here to talk about the *salat* performed by the enlightened ones who have attained the sate of certainty (*yakeen*) but the minimum experience a commoner like myself should have...

Let us first remember...

Muhammad (saw) came to teach us about faith in the **One denoted by the name Allah**, to witness this faith, and to have faith in the **Rasul** who has come to disclose this truth!

If you have understood Muhammad's (saw) message then you would have realized that neither *salat* nor any form of prayer has been advised as offerings to a deity God somewhere in the heavens. For, *there is no such God in the heavens!* And no such God will descend to the earth in the future either!

So, if no form of prayer is done for a God 'out there', then why pray at all?

What is the presence of Allah? What does it mean to be in Allah's presence?

What are we to gain from engaging in such practices?

All enlightened Sufis and saints (*waliyy*), past and present, unanimously agree that **the act of turning to the One denoted by the name Allah pertains to one's essence and the conscious self, or the conscience!**

The conscience is the call of the Reality from one's essence!

---

[12] Quran (107:4-5)

The hadith, **"There are as many ways to Allah as the number of selves in existence"** signifies that the way to attain the reality is not from the outside but from each person's own essence!

Prayer or *salat* is no other than an act of **turning towards the One denoted by the name Allah!**

Prayer is the activation of the structural qualities pertaining to Allah in order to achieve one's wish!

Salat, **for common man, entails the realization and the experience of the various compositional qualities of Allah, such that it can be applied throughout one's daily life even after performing** *salat.*

I shared my thoughts on what I believe *salat* signifies on higher levels in *The Essential Principals of Islam*.

The first thing we recite when we stand for *salat* is "***Subhanaka***", as a reminder of the magnificence and the infiniteness of the One denoted by **the name Allah**, and the insignificance of our world in respect of this grandeur! Evidently, **it is imperative to know what these recitations mean in order to contemplate them and discern the importance and seriousness of their meanings.**

Next, we read the "*Audhu...*" to seek protection, with '*B'illahi*, from the illusion of thinking we are this physical body and thus becoming blinded to many truths.

After this we read the *Basmalah* as "*B-ismi-Allah*"[13] and then we **READ** the chapter **al-Fatiha**...

The word '*hamd*' in al-Fatiha is used to denote '**evaluation**.' So "*hamd* **belongs to Allah**" actually means "**evaluation and appraisal belongs to Allah.**" Indeed, the ability to duly appraise creation of the One denoted by the name Allah belongs only to Him! It is impossible for creation to do this! Thus, at the very beginning, **man is informed of his capacity and cautioned to live within the System without transgressing his boundary!**

---

[13] Please refer to my book *Muhammad's Allah*, available at www.ahmedhulusi.org/en for a detailed explanation of the Basmalah.

Now I want to expound on a different aspect in regards to **Rahman** and **Rahim**...

The word **Rahman** is a proper noun, and therefore, cannot be translated![14]

"Albeit 'Rahman' can inadequately be interpreted as 'the most compassionate' it cannot be translated as such. The mercy and compassion pertaining to Allah is not a sensation of the heart or an emotion of kindness resulting from an inclination felt within the self. As delineated in al-Fatiha, it is a divine will and an infinite blessing."[15]

Life is the essence of every good and blessing. *Rahman* creates us by bringing us into existence with our bodies and spirits, from nothingness, with divine will. Furthermore, He possesses an all-embracing grace with which He provides all of the bounties we need to sustain our lives and enable our continuation.

Based on this, *Rahman*, is far beyond the classical concepts devised by humanly evaluations, such as *protector* and *forgiver*! Universally, it means the One who brings into existence from nothingness, the One who manifests as He wills!

Rahim is the creator of the mechanism through which this is systematically achieved! The word *Rahim* is an Arabic word by origin, which literally means *womb*. Hence, just like how the mother's womb uniquely nourishes and develops the baby to a worldly level of maturity, *Rahim* renders possible the manifestation of *Rahman*'s will, with the names and qualities of the One denoted by the name Allah.

Therefore, **every individual is a creation of *Rahman* and *Rahim*! That is, every individual manifestation is a unique composition of Allah's names, composed by the qualities of *Rahman* and *Rahim*!**

This is the universal meaning of these names. It should not be confused with the perceptions based on worldly and humanly values.

---

[14] Elmalili Hamdi Yazir, *The Interpretation of the Quran*, Volume 1, p32
[15] Elmalili Hamdi Yazir, *The Interpretation of the Quran*, Volume 1, p33

Why Salat?

Especially if we keep in mind that at any given moment one creature is attacking and slaughtering another one, an all merciful God watching over His creation from the heavens seems awfully incongruent with reality!

Needless to say, our understanding of Allah, religion and *sunnatullah* as expounded by Muhammad (saw) seriously needs to be updated in light of our understanding and comprehension today.

What must man, who has been created as the result of the intrinsic qualities denoted by the names *Rahman* and *Rahim*, remember and experience at least five times a day through *salat*?

Man, who has been created with the qualities denoted by Allah's Names, whose essential reality is comprised of these very attributes, must remember that he is not the body to deteriorate away after death, but that he is a conscious being who will live forever as the requisites and the consequences of the potentials within his essence. And the body he will use after his life on earth is called the 'spirit'.

It is the necessity of *Rahim* that man comprehends his reality; discovers the potentials deriving from the Names of Allah within his own essence, and experiences them to gain certainty and attain the station of 'closeness'.

As a result of this, he lives the manifestation of the Maleekiyyah and Malikiyyah[16] in the 'now' and the forever, governed by the decrees of religion – *sunnatullah* (*yawm ad-Din*)!

In order to experience this, one must receive guidance from within their own essence.

This is why we say 'guide us' in al-Fatiha!

We ask to be guided and directed to the path of those who have been given '*in'am*', that is, those who have been enabled to experience the realities within their essence. And we seek protection from becoming of those who deny this reality, and fall

---

[16] Maleek: The Sovereign One, who manifests His Names as He wishes and governs them in the world of acts as He pleases. The one who has providence over all things. Malik: The Absolute Owner

into misconceptions (that lead them away from) reality, and hence become deprived from their essence.

Then we recite some additional verses from the **Quran**, and contemplate on their meanings…

I hope this has answered the question "What is *salat*?" to some extent, even if it is only at a surface level.[17]

I refrain from expanding further as I do not believe the time and place is appropriate. I advise those who want a deeper understanding of *salat* to practice contemplation on what these meanings yield…

Doubtlessly, this topic is exceedingly deep and what I have shared here barely touches the tip of the iceberg.

I believe it is a good idea to reconsider the meaning of the words of **Allah's Rasul: "The deeds between two *salats* will be forgiven"** and try to discern why this may be so…

Again, let us remember the verse:

"So woe to those who pray (due to tradition)**, who are heedless** (cocooned) **of** (the experience of the meaning of) **their** *salat* (which is an ascension [*miraj*] to their innermost essential reality; their *Rabb*)**".**

20 January 2005
Raleigh – NC, USA

---

[17] For more information please refer to the '*Salat*' section in *The Essential Principals of Islam*.

18

FAITH IN MUHAMMAD (saw)

Without a doubt, he who has no faith in Muhammad (saw) **has no faith in Allah! Though he may well believe in his own God!**

Why so?

Because there is no **'God'**! There has never been a 'God'!

Surely, there are imaginary gods in people's minds. In fact, the majority of the people in the world, who identify with various different belief systems, all have such a god in their minds! But these postulations are absolutely incorrect and have no relevance to the reality.

Muhammad (saw) served to warn people against wasting their lives based on their fanciful god-concepts, alerting those who had faith in him to the reality of *"La ilaha..."*[18]

In the past, when people talked of a God in the heavens and his 'son' who has descended to earth, or of angels with wings, the Rasul of Allah denounced these concepts precisely and concisely with the chapter **al-Ikhlas**.

---

[18] I have covered the topic of how and why 'Allah' is not a heavenly God in full scope in my book *Muhammad's Allah*.

Belief in a heavenly God will only lead to suffering! For, such a belief forms an expectation from a being *beyond*. This in turn leads to apathy, sluggishness and laziness! Whereas the truth is, everything is present within the enigma of man's own essence! Not outside! With this mystery, man has the capacity and capability to do many things and at any time.

When those who believe in an external God find out He doesn't actually exist, this disappointment is only going to cause profound suffering for them!

There has never been a God in space, or in another galaxy, who sent messengers or a SON to earth!

Henceforth, the faith of those who believe in Muhammad (saw) and the One denoted as 'Allah' expounded by him, is different to and incongruent with the faith of those who believe in an imaginary external God.

Evidently then, those who do not have faith in Muhammad (saw) and who do not accept and confirm him to be Allah's Rasul and Nabi, do not have faith in 'Allah' as disclosed by Muhammad (saw) either. This means, those who do not accept and confirm Muhammad (saw) as Allah's Rasul, believe in a God based on their own postulations and lead a life proceeding from these conjectures.

Muhammad (saw) said: *"Men kale la ilaha illaAllah fakad dahala jannah!"* That is, **"He who says *'La ilaha illa Allah'* will enter paradise!"**

This does not mean those who believe in a 'God' will enter paradise.

There is a subtle point here:

Muhammad (saw) is hinting to the necessity of **cleansing one's self from the concept of godhood**. In other words, from **duality** (*shirq*)...

Anyone who comprehends the true meaning of chapter *al-Ikhlas* will know there is **no God outside and beyond!**

The **Quran** is filled with verses that state **godhood leads to duality** and dualists will remain in hell forever. What could be the reason for this? Since there is no God, why will the dualists remain in hell and burn forever?

This is an important point to consider and understand!

He who does not have faith in Muhammad (saw) and does not **bear witness** that he is the **Rasul** and **Nabi** of **Allah**, could not have truly have accepted the religion of Islam and *sunnatullah* (System and Order) disclosed by the Rasul of Allah! Thus, one who hasn't accepted this System and Order will only live according to their own conjectures and will have to face the consequences!

No one can put anyone into heaven or cast anyone into hell!

Everyone shapes their own hell or adorns their own heaven with their own capacity of comprehension and the lifestyle they choose for themselves!

He who does not have faith in Muhammad (saw) and does not testify that he is the Rasul and Nabi of Allah cannot recognize and comprehend the One denoted as Allah, as disclosed by Muhammad (saw). This will automatically lead him to believe in a God he creates and adorns in his mind, which in time he will begin to dislike, find faults with and criticize!

The laws and principles of this system, some of which we perceive and understand while some of which we don't, are referred to as *sunnatullah* in the Quran. It is the **System and Order** that we have come to know as **'Religion'**.

Based on the holographic reality, all of the universes are present within every single atom!

The Rasul of Allah shared this knowledge approximately 1,400 years ago with his words: **"The part mirrors the whole"**.[19]

All of the universes have come about from a single 'point' and they function according to the laws of *sunnatullah*.

Like the angle formed from a single point on the shape of the letter 'K', all the universes are contained within a single angle... But

---

[19] Please refer to *The Observing One* for more information on this topic.

on the vertical line forming the letter 'K' there are countless other points! Beyond this is unfathomable! The least we can think of in reference to the existence denoted by the name 'Allah' is this greatness!

Thus, the One denoted by the name 'Allah' is such magnificence that assuredly He is far and beyond the concept of godhood!

To provide a visual depiction, all individual manifestations can be viewed as separate cones. But some only recognize the two-dimensional shape of the cone alone, and think of themselves as flesh and bone. While others recognize the three-dimensionality of the cone and observe the Dimension of the Names (the realities that comprise the essence of existence) all the way back to the apex of the cone, the 'point' of origin!

What we must do is have faith in the Rasul of Allah and the One he disclosed to us as 'Allah', so that we can shape our lives accordingly!

When those who believe in the Rasul of Allah, Muhammad (saw), and the reality he taught as: "There is no God. There is only Allah" pray together, the *Imam* never recites the *Basmalah* aloud; he begins the recitation from the verse '*Alhamdu...*'

Why?

Because the *Basmalah* contains the secret of the letter 'B', which means every individual has to READ and experience the '*B-asmalah*' based on the mystery within their own essence!

Salat can only be experienced by **READING al-Fatiha**, this is why the **Rasul of Allah** asserts **"*Salat* cannot be without al-Fatiha."**

The path to Allah is not an external one that goes to 'beyond', it is an internal one, from one's consciousness to his essence!

Believing in an external God means turning towards the sky or space!

This has nothing to do with culture or race! The word '**Allah**' is a **proper noun**, it is a name! And no name can be translated into another language! It can only be used as it is!

I have no further point to make to those who still fail to see the difference between the name Allah and the general concept of 'God'!

4 March 2005
Raleigh – NC, USA

19

THE FOOTSTEPS OF GOD!

Previously, I had talked about the footsteps of god (!) awaited by the masses. As the author of *Spirit, Man, Jinn*, the only book published in its genre in 1972, I would like to further expand on this topic in light of the changing circumstances...

If the minor signs of Doomsday that Muhammad (saw) mentioned have already come to pass and it is now time for the major signs to appear...

If the 26,000 year cycle of change pertaining to earth, mentioned by Ibrahim Hakki Erzurumi in his *Book of Gnosis* (*Marifatname*) is to be completed in this century...

If the **Mujaddid** (Reviver) of the last century, who comes in the beginning of every Islamic Hijri century, is the final one... That is, if the *Mujaddid* who has come during the Hijri years 1401–1410 was the final *Mujaddid* and he is known as '***al-Mahdi***' and if, according to record, he is only going to be recognized when he appears during a pilgrimage season (*Hajj*) in Mecca some time...

Then let us know that...

Just as the 'knowledge of the *Mahdi* period' is becoming apparent on earth before the *Mahdi* himself, similarly, the 'application of the

Antichrist (*Dajjal*) period' is also apparent and active on earth today. Now it is time for the actual persons to appear.

Based on narrations of various hadith that state that **"the *jinn* are going to be visible to all of mankind"** the 'Messiah Antichrist' is going to emerge under an alien identity **disguised** as the savior, and claim to **be the God (!) of all people!** This is going to be followed by the emergence of Jesus Christ (as)?

Meteor showers, referenced as **"Stones are going to rain down from the skies"**, and narrations **implying an increase in earthquakes and other natural disasters such as "three regions, one in the east, one in the west and one in the middle are going to be destroyed"** are going to be prior to the emergence of the *jinn*, who are going to serve as the **Antichrist's army**. How they are going to do this, only those who live to see it will know…

I want to explain something here:

The word **'*jinn*'** literally means **'an invisible being'**, i.e. invisible to the human eye. Based on this general meaning, **'any and all conscious beings that are invisible to the human eye'** are categorized as the *jinn*. Whether they live on earth, another planet within the solar system or elsewhere in space! **Abdulkadir Al-Jili** talks about the seven different species of *jinn* within seven dimensions, in his work, ***The Perfect Man***. The **Rasul of Allah** (saw) had caught one from one of these types and had let it go. I am not going to go into the details of this now, as this is not our topic. Those who may wish to can research it.

In the same way that in the not so distant past, humanity was ignorant enough to claim that the earth is flat, the sun, moon and all the stars rotate around the earth… Today, the majority of flesh-bone bodied conscious beings called 'humans', who think of themselves as 'intellectuals', still deny **the possibility of other intelligent beings in the universe**… But just as claiming the earth is flat is defective, so is the assumption that humans are the only intelligent beings in the solar system, especially in the entire galaxy!

The fact that mankind can only visually perceive 4-7 ten-thousandth of a centimeter of wavelengths and thus can only accept those within this range as 'existence' is an outdated and backward notion!

Let alone five, today science is asserting the possibility of our brain having 32 sensory inputs! Just as I said in 1972, science is now claiming our brains are not only evaluating wavelengths that are perceived through our eyes but also those that are much beyond these mediums.

Indeed, just as conscious invisible beings dwell among us today, maybe a few years later a different species from another system will come to earth as the army of the **'Messiah'** (!) and pervert humanity toward misguided goals.

The only defense mechanism man has against this *Dajjal* disguised as the Messiah and his army is PRAYER and the reality of *LA ILAHA ILLALLAH*!

One who understands the actual meaning of Muhammad's (saw) declaration *"LA ILAHA"* will know with certainty that no being, oblivious of whatever seeming supernatural power they may exhibit, can ever be a God, and the concept of godhood is invalid, hence will refuse to submit to such figures.

While the *Dajjal* will introduce himself as 'the Father **who sent Jesus' to non-Muslims**, he will introduce himself as the 'Reality' (*Haqq*) to Muslims and demand their submission through ultimatums like "There is no other than the Reality to be worshipped in my being. I am the Reality (*Haqq*). I have become manifest to you here. He who does not prostrate to me will have denied the Reality (*Haqq*)"!

But it has been revealed with certainty that there is no deity God! The concept of godhood is invalid and obsolete. The 'Reality' (*Haqq*) is equally present in every instance of manifestation! **For a single individual to claim he is the Reality and ask others to prostrate to him is no more misleading than to claim** white is black and black is white. **In other words,** it is an attribute of the Antichrist *Dajjal*, **it is deceitful and fraudulent**!

Multiple universes comprising billions of galaxies have all derived their existence from the knowledge, with the knowledge and in the knowledge of Allah!

The path to Allah, for man and all creation, is an inward one, one that goes to one's essence, to one's own reality, not outside!

He who turns to an **outward God** that is 'beyond' is only turning to his own **imagined** conjecture!

The intimates of reality, the **Sufis**, all claim that existence constitutes dimensions within dimensions, the end point of which is the realization and experience of the **individual's nothingness in respect of the One within their essence**!

While pantheism asserts the existence of the individuals and the integrity of the universe, Sufism denounces individual separate existence in respect of the ONE (*AHAD*). The Sufis claim reality can only truly be attained once the individual is cleansed from their ego, i.e. when they realize they do not have a separate existence.

The biggest punishment for an individual, both in this world and in hell, is being veiled from Allah in His essence. In other words it is desolation!

Even the holographic universe model proposed by modern science, claims the ONEness and the non-existence of existence in respect of the creative power (*Qudrah*) within the system of strings or waves.[20]

Hence, based on all of the above, neither the *jinn* from earth or space who will become visible to the whole of humanity, nor the Antichrist *Dajjal* who will perform extraordinary acts with the help of the *jinn*, can be God.

Perhaps in the past such extraterrestrial beings introduced themselves as gods to the people on earth and were recorded in history through various narrations as 'the visit or descent of the gods'... but none of this can mean a God or gods came to earth or created man!

Just as certain troublesome and erroneous tendencies, ambition and selfish leaps, satanic thoughts and feelings, can arise from man's own make-up; it can also be derived from external waves that permeate through him.

---

[20] Please refer to *The Observing One* for more information.

As such, the most effective and fruitful practice man can do is to activate his **prayer mechanism**.

Prayer is the act of turning to the One denoted by the name Allah, to actualize one's aspirations, through the strength and power of Allah!

There is a very subtle yet a crucially important point to take notice of here. I will share this secret in hope that perhaps some day after I am gone, some may remember this knowledge and send me a prayer...

In line with what I said in a previous chapter about why *salat* cannot be without *al-Fatiha*, when an individual seeks protection... They seek it not from an outside source, but **from within their own essence!**

In the transmission from their essence to their consciousness, various dimensions of existence, such as *Ahadiyyah* (Oneness), the station of *Ama* (Nothingness), *Wahdaniyyah* (Unity), *Rahmaniyyah* (the Quantum Potential), *Arsh* (Throne), *Rububiyyah* (compositional qualities denoted by the Names comprising one's essence) and *Ubudiyyah* (i.e. the servitude of the 'self' or individual consciousness), are all present within the individual's essence.

This is very similar to how within the body we have the dimension of cells, within the cells the dimension of genes, within the genes the dimension of proteins, within the proteins the molecules, then the atoms, the waves and ultimately the strings... Each of these dimensions has a sense of consciousness based on its own structural qualities, and all of these stations, states, dimensions exist according to the capacity of the perceiver...

Thus, when one recites a prayer with the intention to seek protection, they are seeking refuge in the strength and power pertaining to the **One denoted by the name Allah** within their own essence. They are **activating and manifesting these qualities**, and as such, forming a field of magnetic waves emanating from their brain as a protective shield.

For example, when we read the **Ayat al-Qursi**, we are actually remembering that the rank or station denoted by '*kursi*' (the Footstool) is in our own '*sama*', that is, our own consciousness,[21] and rules over our own '*ardh*' (body). Hence, we are invoking the strength and power pertaining to the existence of Allah!

So, when you read the various protective prayers advised in *A Guide to Prayer and Dhikr*, such as **al-Falaq** and **an-Nas** in order to be protected from the *jinn*, or ill willed people casting negative energies, you are in fact invoking your own essence for protection! When you start reciting **"Audhu biRabbil falaq..."** or **"Audhu biRabbin nas..."** you are seeking refuge in the attribute of *Rububiyyah* within the Dimension of the Names that comprise your essence, and asking it to protect you, thereby emanating protective brainwaves to expel the negative waves surrounding you. Please try to understand this! For there is no more I can disclose in regards to this topic.[22]

If the prayers for protection are read with the awareness of this mechanism they will certainly be a lot more effective in our lives. Who knows the extent of knowledge that can be revealed if the Quran was read with such awareness!

This is why faith in the One denoted by the name 'Allah', that is, the One who brought into existence 'the existence you presume you have', can never be a God outside or beyond you!

The key to the infinite treasure within our essence is the knowledge and **comprehension of Allah, as disclosed by Muhammad** (saw).

May this comprehension and evaluation be eased and facilitated for us!

The path to a true savior lies in **READing** and understanding the knowledge imparted by Muhammad (saw)!

---

[21] The seven stations of the *nafs* (self)
[22] More information on the topics of *Rabb-Rububiyyah* and 'man as the composition of the names of Allah' can be found in *The Mystery of Man*

I am sure the intimates of the reality (*ahlul haqiqah*) already have insight to this knowledge more profoundly than what has been shared here…

15 April 2005
Raleigh – NC, USA

20

READING THE TREASURE MAP

One day a farmer found a note wrapped in plastic as he was ploughing his field that read: "Read this to find treasure!"

But the writing that followed was in a foreign language so the farmer took it to the *Imam* of his village, who according to the farmer was a great man, perhaps even the saint of their time!

The *Imam* had completed the Quran courses and was familiar with the Arabic alphabet, so he read the note and said: "It says 'Read this to find treasure' and there is a prayer here in Arabic! We must make as many copies of this prayer and give it out to everyone in the village at once!"

So, with his holy hands, the *Imam* rewrote the prayer over and over again and gave a copy to each household in the village!

Now everyone was reciting the 15 line prayer the *Imam* had written in their alphabet.

After some time, the *Imam* announced: "My dear villagers, it seems reciting this prayer once a day is not doing us any good, let us start reciting it once in the morning and once again at night... Surely, there must be some miracle to this!"

After some more time, they decided to recite it 40 times a day, then 100 times a day... And so on...

The Essence of Man

Naturally, some began to complain: "This isn't working…" "There is no treasure!"

"This is nonsense!" "It's a hoax!"

While others eagerly persevered… Months went by, but no treasure was found… Then one day, a traveler stopped by their village. After the evening prayer at the mosque, he realized the congregation was reciting a prayer he had never heard before. He approached the *Imam* as he was leaving the mosque and asked him for a copy of the prayer.

At night, after everyone had gone home, the man lit up a candle in the guesthouse in which he was staying and started to read (!) the Arabic prayer (!) on the paper the *Imam* had given him.

With the candle in one hand and the paper in the other, he walked out of the guesthouse, and went to the enormous sycamore tree in the center of the village. Reading on, he walked towards the stream near the north exit of the village, then again he read the Arabic prayer (!), and went near the willow tree drooping over the streambed. Following the instructions of the prayer (!) he turned his face towards the village, took 21 steps, and began to dig beneath the stone he found there…

Soon after he found a wooden box full of gold coins! He took the box of gold and continued his journey…

The 'prayer' the villagers had been reciting for months was an authentic treasure guide! The only problem was that the villagers had been merely repeating it with no conscious understanding of it! The traveller, on the other hand, **READ it, understood it and applied it**, and found the treasure! While the villagers continued reading the prayer the *Imam* had written for them in their alphabet without having any idea about what they were actually reading!

Yes, they read…

Just like the peasant followers of the *Imam*…

They read for the sake of reading…

Or they try to read, or they can't read…

In *A Guide to Prayer and Dhikr*, I talked about how "even if one does not know the meaning of a particular prayer or *dhikr* they recite, it will still benefit them." For, this pertains to the functioning of this mechanism and its result has nothing to do with belief or a deity in the heavens!

But, how to actually READ?

Those who believe in Muhammad (saw) will believe in and understand the One whose name is Allah, based on the information provided in chapter al-Ikhlas.

Or they will become cognizant of the holographic universe, which will also lead them to the same reality! (For those who have been unjustly accusing me of claiming 'Allah is energy' note that I have said it will *lead* them to the same reality, I did not say it *is* the same reality. Please stop belittling yourselves!)

Based on everything I shared in previous chapters, it is evident that the essence of man comprises the dimension of *Rububiyyah* and his own *Rabb*, whose existence is derived from the Names of Allah! This 'dimension' is not an external spatial dimension but within the very structure connecting his essence to his consciousness! Since this applies to all beings, we say the *Rabb* of the Worlds!

In accordance with the holographic reality, every unit of existence present in the knowledge of the POINT comprising the multiple universes, the *Arsh* (the Throne), the *Kursi* (the Footstool), and all of the heavens and their inhabitants are contained!

Man, who has been created from nothingness, is essentially still inexistent, as only the One called 'Allah' that Muhammad (saw) spoke of exists! This is why the declaration "*La ilaha* – there is no God or godhood" was made!

As such, man is advised to resort to his own reality, that is, to the dimensional qualities pertaining to the **Rububiyyah**[23], **Malikiyyah**[24] and **Ilahiyyah**[25] attributes of Allah within his own essence!

---

[23] The qualities of the Names comprising one's essence
[24] The quality of the Sovereign One, who manifests His Names as he wishes and governs them in the world of acts as He pleases. The one who has providence over all things.
[25] Divine qualities

"**...And He is with you** (the origin of your being) **wherever you are** (as your reality exists with His Names)… (This points to the unity of existence beyond the illusion of duality)." (Quran 57:4)

Hence:

"**And if you speak your thoughts** (or conceal them,) **know that indeed He knows the secret** (in your consciousness) **and what is even deeper** (the actual Names that compose it)." (Quran 20:7)

This is because you are not praying to something outside and beyond you!

The *Malik* in al-Fatiha also points to this:

"*Iqra kitabak kafa bi nafsikal yawma alayka hasiba*".

"**READ the knowledge** (book) **of your life! Sufficient is your self** (your consciousness) **against you at this stage as an accountant** (witness the results of your thoughts and actions during your worldly life lest you judge others)." (Quran 17:14)

In line with the holographic reality, the Name '*Hasib*' is present within us at the dimension of *Rububiyyah*. Thus, the act of giving account is not to a God beyond! We give account to the **Malikiyyah of the One named Allah** in our essence on the '*yawm ad-Din*" the 'now' and the forever governed by the decrees of religion – *sunnatullah*. As opposed to some distant day, *centuries away*!

This is why, before the Quran is recited the *ahlul hal* (the ones who experience the reality) say "***B-ismi-ALLAH ar-Rahman ar-Rahim***" to mean "at every instance, my reality becomes manifest with the *Rahman* and *Rahim* qualities of Allah"!

Thus, *salat* is the experience of this reality!

The *Ayat al-Qursi* also emphasizes the various levels and qualities of the One whose name is '**Allah**', present in man's essence, urging man to remember and evaluate them! In contrast to man's sleepy nature, it calls to attention the aspect within his essence that never sleeps.

While the verses that begin with "Say" invite us to read them, they actually encourage the **READ**er to **experience** their meaning.

That is, these verses do not imply that we turn to a heavenly God to seek His help, but rather, that we duly serve the One whose name is '**Allah**' by deservedly discerning the dimensions within our essence comprising our very existence and reality.

Of course, this is my understanding and does not bind anyone...

Unfortunately, I see that sharing my understanding of Allah, as disclosed by Muhammad (saw), has only led some to 'update' their understanding of a glorious God beyond!

Whereas the following verse clearly explicates the invalidity of godhood after believing in the One whose name is Allah:

"**Do not turn to (assume the existence of) a god** (exterior manifestations of power or your illusory self) **besides Allah. For there is no God. Only HU! Everything** (in respect of its thingness) **is inexistent, only the face of HU** (only that which pertains to the Absolute Reality) **exists!**" (Quran 28: 88)

Some did not annihilate their existence; they merely **realized** their inexistence in respect of Allah...

And some created a 'god' to exalt 'themselves' (identities) and become the 'glorified' ones of this world and the hereafter!

Indeed, those who accepted the religion of Islam by realizing their 'inexistence' and accepting the reality that only the One whose name is Allah exists, have read the treasure map brought by Muhammad (saw) and **followed** its instructions. They have read the **Quran** and deciphered **the secrets it signifies**; they have **READ** the One whose name is Allah and the worlds He created with His names and the system and order in which they live, and as a result, they found the infinite magnificent treasure within their essence!

While others squandered away their lives with gossip and hearsay...

As **Yunus** would say: "Another one from the herd passed over…"

6 May 2005
Raleigh – NC, USA

21

MISCONCEPTIONS ON THE ISLAMIC WAY OF LIFE (SUNNAH)

Is the Islamic way of life about beards, headscarves and turbans, and dress codes?

What could the **Sunnah** of **Allah's Rasul** really be about?

What exactly is the Islamic way of life, the **Sunnah of Allah**, or '*sunnatullah*'?

For some, it means an Islamic lifestyle based on growing a beard, having a moustache, and wearing a white dress and turban!

Following the **Rasul of Allah**, for these people, means to employ the dress code of 1,400 years ago, and to apply the customs and traditions of that century! These are the Muslims who claim wearing short-sleeved shirts makes one a blasphemer (*qafir*)!

It was this very understanding that martyred Hadhrat Ali, the pinnacle of sainthood (*wilayah*), the '**door to knowledge**'! This is the kind of understanding that labeled Hadhrat Ali as being blasphemous and anti-religious!

One need only look at the words of Allah's Rasul (saw) in regards to Hadhrat Ali to understand the state and misunderstanding of the

Muslims who killed him for being contrary to **Rasulullah**'s (saw) path!

Discern well those who exploit religion, turning it into a 'sovereignty' in which they reign and rule over the people, all under the guise of 'serving' religion!

As some of my views, which I shared in private company, were somehow published on the internet, I wanted to clarify this topic in person...

Please think seriously about what I am about to tell you!

When I was around 20 years old, approximately 40 years ago, I saw the **Rasul of Allah** (saw) in my dream in which he instructed me to go and see **Hadhrat Abu Bakr**... The rest of it isn't important; suffice it to say, later that year I wrote a book on **Hadhrat Abu Bakr**, and after that, a book called *Muhammad Mustapha* (saw) comprising hadith relating the life of the **Rasul of Allah** (saw) during his years in Mecca.

I mention this because I had thoroughly researched the lifestyle of that time, reading approximately 60 thousand authentic hadith as reference.

Think about this... the **Rasul of Allah**, Muhammad Mustapha (saw), was born into a pagan Quraysh tribe who were idolaters. His grandfather, uncles and all his relatives had the same belief system.

He was born and raised among them, he dressed like them, he grew a beard like they did, he wore a turban as they did, and he sat and walked and ate like them...

This was the lifestyle he had before becoming the **Rasul of Allah**.

At 39, as the **Rasul of Allah**, he became aware of the universal reality. When three years later, his *Nubuwwah* was activated through revelations, he was able to teach the requirements of eternal life.

During this time, he changed neither **his beard, nor the way he dressed!**

He continued to dress and wear a turban like the men in his tribe and kept his beard! He even continued wearing his colorful striped caftan...

The Sunnah of Allah's Rasul is the Sunnah of Allah, to whom he is a Rasul, i.e. it is the *sunnatullah*!

Hence, when we understand and apply the *sunnatullah* we practice the Sunnah of **Rasulullah**, not by growing a beard or wearing a dress and a turban!

It is important to note that the **Rasul of Allah** (saw), neither interfered **with the dress code** of the idolaters, such as Abu Jahl, Abu Lahab and their successor Yazid, who murdered **Rasulullah**'s (saw) grandson, nor did he concern himself with such trivial matters. In fact, he continued to dress and live just like them.

Such things have no relevance or significance to the application of religious requirements, these things have **no pertinence to the reality of an eternal life and the knowledge of the One known as 'Allah'**!

Therefore...

A person who is guided to the reality by Allah may still continue to comply with the customs and traditions of their community, without following them in matters concerning *sunnatullah*; **they can continue to share knowledge regarding matters about which they have received guidance!**

In other words, the Sunnah of the Rasul, far from rejecting the customs and traditions of the community, entails their compliance!

For religion has not come to reform our dress code!

Religion has no business with such insignificant matters!

According to Sunnah, people have the right to dress, read, work and live as they wish, so long as they don't disrupt the peace of their community, despite how controversial and contradictory this may sound to those who fail to understand the mechanics of the brain and are stuck at the level of their body!

To judge someone's faith and religion by their dress code is a conspicuous display of a primitive, underdeveloped thinking and is the output of an imitator brain.

The **Rasul of Allah** (saw) strived to teach the people about the system and order in which they lived. He urged people to comply with the 'system and order of Allah', called 'religion', so they may be **prepared for their eternal lives**.

A 'religious' person means a person who **researches about, understands and complies with the system and order of Allah!** Thus, based on the realities he READs, a religious person is one who 'protects themself' against the dangers of the future.

To follow the Sunnah of Allah's Rasul is to adopt his views and to walk on the path he advises by implementing his recommendations and attaining a graceful future. It is not to waste a lifetime immersed in imitation!

To follow the Sunnah of Allah's Rasul is to share the knowledge he has been endowed with, without expecting anything in return! It is not to distract people with stories of clothing and attire!

One who comprehends and complies with the system and order of Allah, i.e. *'sunnatullah'*, necessarily complies with the **Sunnah of Allah's Rasul!**

The warning **"One who likens himself to a tribe belongs to that tribe"** implies that we belong to the community with which we share the same **'ideology and beliefs'** not the same style of clothing!

Some people have forbidden the questioning and inquisition of religion, thereby yielding an increase in the number of unintellectual brains that operate by memorizing and copying...

The world is the abode of wisdom (*hikmah*) and everything expounded by the **Rasul of Allah** (saw) is based on wisdom. The intellectual is the one who inquires, questions and researches the teachings of **Rasulullah** (saw) in order to decipher the wisdom in his words.

This is why the Rasul of Allah (saw) says: **"Wisdom is the lost property of the believer."**

One who has a discrepancy or a contradiction in their system of thought does not comprehend religion, fails to **READ** the mechanism and lives only as an imitator of the system in which they live. Religion does not accept imitation!

Imitating a physical action may produce the same outcomes, but one cannot imitate **comprehension**!

To be '*faqih*', that is, to be a person of 'understanding', is the blessing and favor of Allah, to free a person from imitation.

Faqih **does not mean one who** *memorizes* **the rules of** *fiqh* **(Islamic law)!**

The invention of the tape recorder outdated that notion decades ago!

Religion has been disclosed to us as a **READable** source, such that we recognize the system and order of which we are a part and our place in it, but most importantly, so that we get to **know ourselves**, **discover the treasure** within our essence, and eventually know the One whose name is Allah in accordance with the holographic reality!

Those who fail to understand this have obviously failed to **read** the chapter al-Ikhlas, though they may have repeated it a hundred thousand times!

Let us take heed of **Rasulullah**'s (saw) words: "Some pray a lot, but their prayer produces nothing other than fatigue, some fast frequently but their fasting yields nothing other than hunger."

The Rasul of Allah (saw) has conveyed the **Quran** so that we understand it and contemplate on it. Thereby, taking each step of our lives in congruence with the '*sunnatullah.*' The Rasul has not come so that we squander our lives bickering and spreading rumors about hair, beards and clothes, and judging people!

What is the true understanding of religion introduced with the creed "There is no God or godhood besides the One denoted by the name Allah (*La ilaha illa Allah*)"?

If one wastes their life in imitation rather than occupying themself with the answer to this question, the consequence of

their failure to read and discover their infinite treasures will be immense suffering and disappointment!

And alas! There is no concept of compensation in the system!

Note: This is my personal understanding and does not bind anyone. Some may wish to share it with others. And some may find it discomforting to their vested interests and forbid my writings because they cause the reader to 'think and contemplate'…

19 May 2005
Raleigh – NC, USA

22

THE CRUX

What is the crux of understanding the Universal System described as the **'Religion of Islam'** and the answers to the questions **"who and what am I?"**

Why are these topics prone to so much misunderstanding?

Why do we get stuck on a frame or two, and fail to see the picture as a whole?

Why can't we deservedly evaluate the **Quran** and observe it with all its lucidity?

These are the questions that emanate from thinking brains! Imitators, who follow blindly and unmindfully, have no such concerns!

To rightfully understand and evaluate the teachings of **Muhammad** (saw) and the Quran we must be fully cognizant of the following two realities:

1. **The universal aspect of the system**
2. **The aspect of the individual's life within the system**

The Sufi practices, which entail the deep contemplation, experience and application of these realities, talks of two types of observation:

1. **Sayr-i afaqi** (the recognition of the universal realities)
2. **Sayr-i anfusi** (the recognition of the individual realities)

The first of these **observations** is the realization of the **Universal System and Order**, created in the knowledge of the **One whose name is Allah**. The second one is the affiliation of the individual with the **reality** of their self (*nafs*).

The Quran attenuates the realities that must be recognized both in respect of the *sayr-i afaqi* and the *sayr-i anfusi* throughout many of its verses. If we take into account only one of these observations, we will be deprived of the other aspect of the matter, and become intellectually deviated.

Why so?

Because as a result of a single misunderstanding, the Quran has been reduced from being the explication of the universal system (*sunnatullah*) and its creator, to **a book of commands of a heavenly God**! Whereas, the intimates of the reality of the past and present have strived to explain the contrary.

I have shared my understanding of the One whose name is Allah, in *Muhammad's Allah*, in a way that has never been approached before. If one can properly understand and evaluate *Muhammad's Allah* they will be able to realize the ways through which the existence of Allah becomes manifest through man, in respect of the holographic reality.

Other than that there is no god or godhood, the reality what Muhammad (saw) tried to communicate to us was who and what the One whose name 'Allah' is! This is what the Quran elucidates! This is why, despite all the criticism I receive by those who are inadequate at READing, I say "the One whose name is Allah" to draw the attention to the fact that 'Allah' is only a name! Hence, we should stop postulating ideas based on a name and contemplate on what the name actually references!

Yes...

The absolute essence (*dhat*) of the **universe** exists with the absolute essence (*dhat*) of the Qayyum One!

But the universe isn't God!

The absolute essence (*dhat*) of **man** exists with the absolute essence (*dhat*) of the *Qayyum* One!

But man is not God!

The **universe** has come into existence with the structural qualities denoted by the names and attributes of Allah, and this will always be so!

Man has come into existence with the structural qualities denoted by the names and attributes of Allah, and this will always be so!

The **universe** is *Hayy* because Allah is *Hayy*[26]!

Man is *Hayy* because Allah is *Hayy*!

The **universe** is conscious, because Allah is *al-Aleem*[27]!

Man is conscious because Allah is *al-Aleem*!

Consciousness is the manifestation of the attribute of knowledge!

Beneath the **'universe'** name and picture is the *Rabb* of the worlds (the source of the infinite meanings of the Names) who brings into existence whatever He desires, and who, as the requisite of His Uluhiyyah manifests Himself with His *Wahidiyyah* (Oneness) and maintains new creation and formation at every instance with His *Rahmaniyyah* (infinite quantum potential)!

Beneath the **'man'** name and picture is the *Rabb* of the worlds (the source of the infinite meanings of the Names) who brings into existence whatever He desires, and who, as the requisite of His *Uluhiyyah* manifests Himself with His *Wahidiyyah* (Oneness) and maintains new creation and formation at every instance with His *Rahmaniyyah* (infinite quantum potential)!

Thus, every state of manifestation in the universe is present at a micro level within man. Man will know the universe to the degree he knows himself...

---

[26] The source of names! The One who gives life to the Names and manifests them. The source of universal energy, the essence of energy!

[27] The One who, with the quality of His knowledge, infinitely knows everything in every dimension with all its facets.

When the reality of *Uluhiyyah* created the essence (*dhat*) of man, He created man as a mirror. He made man *Wahid* with His *Wahidiyyah*, and continually created through him with His *Rahmaniyyah*, and became the *Haliq* (creator) of all his actions with His *Rububiyyah*!

The ***Arsh***, ***Kursi*** and the **seven heavens** and **earth** are within the universe!

The ***Arsh***, ***Kursi*** and the **seven heavens** and **earth** are within man!

The universe exists with all the angels!

Man exists with all the angels!

Those who have been granted '***Marifatullah***', the fourth state after '***Haqiqah***' (Reality), will **READ** and discern well what these metaphors represent within the system. They will know what the *Arsh* and *Qursi* means, and which forces within the system the angels denote!

Hence the saying goes: **"Whatever you seek, seek within yourself"**.

For, if you know yourself as the micro world, you will know the universe as the macro world. Thereby, you will know who and what the '*Rabb* of the worlds' is!

The ***sayr-i anfusi*** (the path of the inward journey) is the process of knowing the self.

The travelers of this path will unavoidably pass through and stop over at the station of 'knowing the self as the Reality.' This will lead them to the pit: "I am the Reality (*Haqq*) I will do as I please, all is legitimate for me." This state is referred to as the ***nafs-i mulhima*** (the inspired self) for the self, in this state, begins to receive inspiration as to its own reality. If one cannot surpass this station and reach the 'content consciousness' state, then the inciting self (***nafs-i ammarah***) will begin to weigh heavier. With the knowledge of the inspired self, the self will begin to develop a pharaoh-like identity and begin perceiving itself as perfect and everybody else as flawed, and in this state it will leave this world!

"So many heads were lost on this path, about which nobody inquired" was said in reference to these losses!

Indeed, man's essence may be comprised of the Reality, but this does not exonerate man from being responsible for his deeds! At every moment, man will inevitably live the consequence of his previous actions! He will compulsorily live the outcome of whatever thought or action he yields!

In other words, today is the result of yesterday.

Now, let us come to the crux of the matter...

Let us try to understand this in light of Hadhrat Abu Bakr's most excellently put words: "**The comprehension that you will never comprehend Allah, is the comprehension of Allah**"...

Everything the Quran expounds in regards to the One whose name is Allah should be evaluated in respect of both the universal aspect (i.e. in terms of the essence and consciousness of the universe) and the aspect pertaining to the existence denoted by the word 'man' and his reality!

As I mentioned above, all of the definitions delineated in the *Ayat al-Qursi*, in the verses beginning with "*Kul audhu*" and "*Kul HuAllahulleziy*" reveal the various qualities of manifestation, both universally and through man.

So what and where is the *Rabb* and the *Malik* in whom we seek refuge then? Where is "*ilahin nas*" to whom we resort?

The **Names of Allah** are the compositional qualities present in the dimension of *Rububiyyah* (the compositional qualities denoted by the Names), both in the universe and in man's existence.

Hence, when we read the **Quran**, we must be cognizant of the fact that everything said **in regards to Allah** denotes the structural compositions, or the qualities, that comprise us. And everything we are to encounter in the future will be in the scope of these qualities!

To sum it up: If we want to understand the **Quran**, first we must keep in mind that the Quran is not a book of commands sent by a God beyond. Then, with the conception that it is the book of the System of Allah, of '*sunnatullah*' and the disclosure of the intrinsic qualities pertaining to the essence of man and the universe denoted by the name 'Allah', we may begin to walk on the path to maturity...

The ultimate and undeniable reality is that the **One whose name is 'Allah'**, is the creator of man and the multiple universes with the compositional qualities denoted by His names, within His knowledge!

But, neither man nor the universe can be deified!

To this day, no truly enlightened **conscious being** has declared to be '**Allah**'!

30 May 2005
Raleigh – NC, USA

23

THE DIFFERENCE OF MUHAMMAD (saw)

The One denoted by the name Allah was disclosed to us by Muhammad (saw) who, **rather than a *prophet*, was the Rasul of Allah**!

What was his exception? How was he different to previous Rasuls?

Abraham (as), **Moses** (as) and **Jesus** (as) were all **Rasuls of Allah** too...

Why is it compulsory to confirm the *Risalah* of Muhammad (saw)?

Why is it implied that if we accept and confirm all other Rasuls but deny Muhammad (saw) we will lose everything?

As the **last and final Nabi**, and the **servant and the Rasul of Allah, Muhammad** (saw) had a uniquely distinctive role to Abraham (as), who brought the concept of *'Hanif'*, and Moses (as), who conveyed *tanzih* (incomparability) and Jesus (as) who taught *tashbih* (similarity). Distinctive to all these, Muhammad (saw) adjoined *tashbih* and *tanzih* and proposed the ultimate: *tawhid* (unity).

Muhammad (saw) **READ** the *sunnatullah*, and through verses and hadith he informed people about everything they need to know based on this system.

Those who claim: "There is no need for hadith, the Quran is sufficient" neither understand the **Quran**, nor evaluate the **signs pertaining to the One whose name is Allah**, nor do they understand the functions of Rasul and Nabi!

They still imagine a great God in the distant space who sends commands via His winged angels to His postman-prophets on earth! They have no idea about who Muhammad (saw) is or what his function is. They do not recognize Muhammad's (saw) disclosure of the magnificent *sunnatullah*, the mechanics of the universal system that embodies the whole of mankind.

Like an android, **they suffice with repeating the Quran** and performing **the physical actions of the *salat* to worship their deity God!** As such, they will pass through this world unaware of their loss! **The incomprehension and unawareness of these realities will be their biggest punishment.**

If the ungrateful one who denies the **Rasul** and claims the Quran is enough were to erase all the knowledge in their memory that they received from the **Rasul of Allah**, will they have anything left at all to say about the **Quran** and the knowledge pertaining to it?

Being ungrateful to the one who enlightens with the knowledge of Allah and *sunnatullah* can only **result in becoming completely and indefinitely veiled to the comprehension and experience of these realities**. And this will not be in the form of a deity God sending punishment from the sky, but as the natural consequence of their own doings administered by their own essence. This occurs as an impediment in the brain, enforced by the mechanics of the system (*sunnatullah*). Any time one denies something they create an impediment between their self and the thing they deny!

The ungrateful ones who think of the Rasul of Allah (saw) as a postman-prophet impede their own paths by succumbing to their nonsensical assumptions.

Muhammad (saw) advised *salat*, which cannot be complete without **READing the al-Fatiha**, in respect of his *Risalah*. His observation of ablution (*wudu*) before performing *salat*, on the other hand, was the necessity of his *Nubuwwah*.[28]

Some compare and liken the recital of **'Bismillah'** and the **'al-Fatiha'** in *salat*, which for the spiritually adept is the experience of ascension (*miraj*), to yoga or the Nirvana concept in Hinduism. Whereas these practices have nothing in common! I will share more on this later.

Muhammad (saw) is **the final Nabi**, because he has revealed all and everything of *sunnatullah* concerning humanity. The topic of **'*sunnatullah*'** is extremely crucial. One who fails to understand *sunnatullah* will never be able to break out of their cocoon; they will continue to live within their imagination. In Sufism, this has been expressed as being in the sleeping state, or **dreaming**. After all, how real is a dream?

Due to the conditions of the century it was revealed in, metaphoric and symbolic language was employed, but today, those with adequate scientific knowledge can ascertain and evaluate Muhammad (saw) in a much different light.

We must realize and accept the following absolute truth:

The **One whose name is Allah** is the One whose name is Allah. And a servant is a servant!

Even if the existence of the servant and everything pertaining to their existence is derived from the One whose name is Allah, the servant is still just a 'servant' and can never be Allah.

Muhammad (saw), despite his magnificent being and knowledge, and the qualities of Allah he manifested, was just a 'servant' (*abd*) and this will always be the case!

The reason for this lies in the words of Muhammad (saw): "**The part is the mirror of the whole.**" This statement says something about **servanthood**.

What is a **servant**?

---

[28] The function of enabling people to read and apply the necessary practices of the system of Allah.

A **servant** is one who must obey the wants of the One denoted by the name Allah.

Let me explain by way of examples:

A single fig consists of the numerous seeds within it. A fig fruit represents unity within multitude; it symbolizes individuality within multiplicity. This is why there is a chapter in the Quran, named "The Fig"…

Furthermore, the **holographic reality** dictates the whole of the universe with all its dimensions is present within every single unit comprising the universe.

Based on this, then, Allah is present within every iota of existence, with His Essence, Attributes, Names, the *Arsh*, *Kursi*, and the seven heavens and earth!

This applies not only to man but to all forms of life in all dimensions![29]

All beings in the universe possess a form of consciousness befitting its own individual make-up, and the dimension and life in which it resides. A being from one dimension cannot perceive a being in another dimension due to its structural properties.

Hence, due to these intrinsic levels within each being, every unit of existence has the opportunity to reach its *Rabb*, *Maleek*[30] and *Ilah* (God) through ascending or leaping between these levels within its essence, like an artesian well, or '*uruj*'.

In some individuals, knowledge flows from their essence like the outburst of water from the source, or a geyser.

Wilayah actualizes through the path of *uruj*. **Risalah**, the highest state of *wilayah* involves the path of *irsal* (disclosure). **Risalah** involves the manifestation of the name **al-Waliyy**, and is expressed on man as the Rasul.

In respect of the value denoted by their *risalah*, all Rasuls are equal. They differ, however, in respect of the attributes comprising

---

[29] More information about this can be found in *The Observing One*.
[30] The Sovereign One, who manifests His Names as he wishes and governs them in the world of acts as He pleases. The one who has providence over all things.

the source of the knowledge disclosed to them. For some, the disclosure occurs from the attribute of Power, for others, from Knowledge or from Life.

Coming back to our topic, despite the manifestation of the attributes and qualities, and the disclosure of *sunnatullah* through and from Muhammad (saw), he is not Allah, he is only a servant (*abd*)!

This applies to all forms of existence, every single iota, in the universe.

The part is the mirror of the whole, but a part can never be the whole, even if the whole exists in the part. A part is a part, not the whole!

He who refers to the whole, which is based on the holographic reality, as the One who is denoted by the name Allah, will have grossly misjudged and will deviate from the reality.

A warning and reminder to those with such tendencies:

"The One whose name is Allah does not accept fragmentation!"

At this point, the meaning of the chapter *al-Ikhlas* should be revised and seriously contemplated. If, due to His *Ahadiyyah* (Absolute Oneness) and *Samadiyyah* (The Absolutely Self-Sufficient and Whole One), no existence can be considered other than Him, then in this respect, even the concept of unity becomes invalid.

As I had previously explained with the example of the letter 'K' in *Muhammad's Allah*, the 11 dimensions of the universe, the parallel universes, or the multi universes, have all manifested in the Knowledge of the One, and comprise the holographic 'whole'. A part is a mirror to this whole!

The Sufis of the past expressed this reality as **'a dream within a dream'**. The point is a dream in the sight of Allah... The whole that projects within the angle of this point is also dream... **Every iota within this whole that mirrors the whole is also dream...!**

This is why, even the whole that is holographically present in the part, cannot be the One denoted by the name Allah. It is only a 'point' emanating as a form of knowledge in His Knowledge!

That is, **the 11 dimensions, or the entire collection of parallel universes, are present within every iota, like the seeds inside a fig.** That is all. And even this is a servant (*abd*) to Allah!

If I have been able to share some insight here then it would have become apparent that the reality is far beyond phrases such as 'I am the Reality' and the erroneous perception that everything is legitimate to us because the Reality (*haqq*) is inside everything and present everywhere!

I have been found guilty of causing confusion and writing of controversial and complicated topics. I direct such people to reading books about the laws of Islam or the stories of saints!

Apologies, thus is the expression of my servanthood!

I beg you, pray for me if you may, but do not be upset with this humble servant for sharing the knowledge of Allah as disclosed by **Muhammad** (saw) without wanting anything in return…

13 June 2005
Raleigh – NC, USA

24

OUT WITH THE OLD AND IN WITH THE NEW

The farmer had grown accustomed to plowing his fields with his old tractor. He had no complaints. He enjoyed his tractor so much he even performed sophisticated (!) artistic tricks with it…

One day, his son, who was an electromechanical expert, arrived from Germany with one of the latest vehicles. The old farmer was mesmerized! The vehicle worked with electronic buttons, it went on land and water, it even levitated a couple of meters to overcome obstacles!

He thought: "Easy… It's just another vehicle like my tractor… I can use that, too…"

His son warned him: "Father, you can only use this vehicle for the specific purpose it has been created for, as outlined in its instruction manual. Every system has its own instruction manual. If you want performance from this vehicle, you have to comply with its manual!"

The old farmer did not like this warning.

"I have been using a tractor for 50 years! I know perfectly well how to use a vehicle! Just give it to me and let me test drive it!"

Needless to explain what happened next. You can guess the rest…

For years I have been writing about the universal order and the system of life called '*sunnatullah*'. For years I have been striving to expound that everything works with a specific system, and a cause and effect relation.

There is no magic wand in the hands of a God in space!

Life is subject to constant renewal, and at every level will forever be so!

If this were not the case there would not be a Reviver (*mujaddid*) in every century.

But this isn't our topic... Our topic is about how and by who the new expositions will be evaluated.

Allow me to give an example from myself:

On 13 September 1963, I began to employ various Islamic practices such as *dhikr* and *salat*. I must admit these initial applications were no more than imitation and were based on my limited understanding at the time. But as time went on, I continually inquired into the reason and wisdom of all these practices. I asked what, why and how? I commenced a thorough research... I began with the interpretation of the Quran by Elmalili Hamdi Yazir, then went on to the Sahih Bukhari collection of hadith, and then read other hadith books. At the beginning of 1964 I met the late **Sayyid Osman Efendy of Madina**, and acquired various techniques of prayer and *dhikr* from him.

After this I began to explore Sufism. I read almost **everything from Abdulqadir Jilani and Muhyiddin Ibn Arabi to Ahmad Rufai and Abdulkareem al-Jili**. I benefited and learned the views of all these eminent scholars. I applied all the spiritual techniques they advised to the best of my ability. In 1965 I had the opportunity to go to *hajj* (pilgrimage) and on my return I wrote my first book: *Prayer*.

Then I had to do my military service... In 1967, I penned my book *Revelations* based on my views and comprehension in that particular period of time.

I began to spend my days in prayer and fasting. There were times when I observed certain spiritual diets that lasted 80–120 days, and times when I spent 4–5 days consecutively fasting (with nothing to eat or drink). There were no practices that I read about or heard of that I didn't put into practice!

In the meantime, I was introduced to the importance **of Allah's 'Mureed' attribute. I saw that man's biggest weakness was related to the deactivation of the attribute of will, which became activated in the brain with the constant repetition (*dhikr*) of the name *Mureed*.** According to my understanding, the repetition of this name has an effect on the brain's biochemistry first, then its bioelectricity, and eventually the 'spirit'. The late Ghazali mentioned the importance of the name *Mureed* in many of his books.

Some people began to gossip, claiming this name was a fabrication I was using to draw an audience, and that it wasn't really one of Allah's names because it wasn't listed among the **99 Names**. I responded to these with a smile and went on my way. For they were so ignorant as to not know that ***Mureed* was the name of one of Allah's Seven Essential Attributes, the attribute of will!**

Whatever knowledge I have acquired in my life, I first applied it to myself and in my own life, then recommended it to those around me.

Ultimately, years of practice proved to me that the *dhikr* of the names '*Mureed*', '*Quddus*' and '*Fattah*' has profound effects in the brain. I published these formulas in my book *Prayer* under the section "**Special *Dhikr***".

My observations showed me that the continual *dhikr* of these and other **Names of Allah** resulted in significant changes in people in terms of their perception and comprehension. They were able to grasp and understand many mysteries to which they had no prior insight. Of course, given that their intellectual condition and natural disposition and capacity allowed them.

This was an activation of a mechanism in the brain!

It had nothing to do with whether the person believed or not…

It merely involved the operation of a mechanism Allah embedded in man's brain!

I witnessed many of my **Alawi or atheist** acquaintances practice *dhikr* **without 'believing'** and achieve the same results.

Eventually, I penned some of my knowledge based on these experiences in *A Guide to Prayer and Dhikr* to share it with those who may be interested.

New things are produced by new methods. Old methods cannot yield new results!

My new way was the repetition of these names in the brain. All the results were in relation to the meanings of these three names...

Other than *dhikr*, I also advise *tasbih salat* and a particular *salat* recommended by **Muhammad** (saw) to his uncle. There are numerous hadith on fasting and the importance of **maintaining ablution at all times**. There are many verses and narrations in regards to the necessity of **performing *salat* duly and deservedly rather than as an imitation**. The **consecutive fasting** I practice and advise some of my close friends are not for everybody anyway. Compulsory fasting is only for the month of Ramadan. Other than that, fasting on the days of a full moon, or Mondays and Thursdays, has also been advised... **Ismail Hakki Bursawi** talks about those who fast consecutively for 7, 11 or 40 days but these are very eminent people. I do not think it would be appropriate for me to imitate them!

I wrote about all the compulsory prayers and their reasons in *The Essential Principles of Islam*. Those who may be interested in learning the wisdom behind these practices may refer to it.

My genuine intent was to explain to you that new achievements cannot occur via old and tried methods; a new attainment can only be acquired through a new technique. The old can never produce the new!

To read and talk about Sufism, even if systematically, without engaging in the prayers and other spiritual practices, cannot be considered anything more than a 'hobby.' It will remain only as a philosophy!

Reading and writing about the philosophy of Sufism does not make one a Sufi!

Repeating the ways of yesterday won't take anyone further than yesterday.

Hadhrat Ali, the pinnacle of *Wilayah*, says: **"Raise your children for tomorrow, not for today!"**

The Divine Book sustains its newness and originality until Doomsday, yet appropriately addresses the people of the past according to their time. Shame on us if we still understand and interpret the Quran in respect to the past!

I write these because... I have come to be 60 years of age... I have two years left to the age at which **Rasulullah** (saw) left this world... I do not know how long I will live with a healthy brain and intellect... I am not a sheikh or a murshid... **I do not claim to be a guru or a master of any kind... I do not have labels... I have no rank or position and do not expect anybody's recognition...** The reason I wrote these things was to help you understand that without engaging in any spiritual practice one cannot achieve significant insight... I am an ordinary thinker who shares his thoughts only with those who are interested... Those who benefit from my views will continue to read my work, and those who find my views contradictory to their existing database can go ahead and live their life as they wish...

I believe I was facilitated by Allah to acquire new insight involving certain new practices (in relation to the three names I mentioned above). And because of this, I say... **Every new formation is founded on a new approach. This applies to today and to tomorrow! Even if one has the skill and capacity**, with a traditional approach one cannot generate anything but a traditional result.

Religion is the name of Allah's system. In order to thoroughly discover and evaluate this system, together with all its sublimity and mysteries, one must employ new means in a systematic way!

One cannot dig a well by grubbing the garden a little here and a little there! The fickle one who claims: "there is no water in this garden" after such a whimsical approach will only cause damage to themself.

I am impotent in duly thanking... My *Rabb* has facilitated and allowed me to realize my servitude and nothingness...

I have no interest in the gossip of other people. The smart one will not waste their time with my gossip, but make the best of their life by engaging in useful practices.

When my time comes, He is going to take me away from my village and enable me to commence a new life, in another dimension...

"We depart from this place, and say '*salaam*' to those who stay" as Yunus would say...

I have shared with your servants, **without any material gain**, the knowledge you have disclosed to me; as much as you have allowed me to... They are your servants! The judgment is yours alone, O *Rabb* of the worlds!

17 June 2005
Raleigh – NC, USA

25

SUNNATULLAH
(The Immutable Constants of Allah's System)

The biggest miracle of the One denoted by the name Allah is Muhammad Mustapha (saw)! His brain and his reality, and the communication between his brain and his reality, are the biggest miracles that have occurred on earth!

And the biggest miracle of **Allah's servant and Rasul**, Muhammad (saw), is the Quran!

Why?

Because, as the **Rasul** and **Nabi of Allah**, no one that has come before him and none that will follow him has or can disclose the knowledge he has disclosed! Thus, there will be no more **Nabi** after him.

What is his miraculous disclosure?

The **Quran** comprises two intricate themes or categories:

1. The denouncing of **God and godhood** and the enouncing of the One denoted by the name Allah. (This is the topic of *Risalah*)

2. The proclamation of the **universal system and order** known as '*sunnatullah*,' and based on this, a guide to the practices

and the abstinences that should be observed to achieve beneficial results for man. (This is the area that concerns **Nubuwwah**)

All the laws with which we automatically comply in this world and all the universal laws have been termed '*sunnatullah*' in the Quran...

Everything from the movement of quantum strings and the holographic reality, to relations between universes, the integral energy of the universe, the cosmological relations, and the Arsh, Kursi and the seven heavens and earth within the essence of man, occur in the scope of *sunnatullah*!

Sunnatullah has been described as:

"**...And you will not find in our sunnah any change.**" (Quran 17:77)

"**...And never will you find in the System** (course) **of Allah** (*sunnatullah*) **any change.**" (Quran 48:23)

"**...You will never encounter an alternative for *sunnatullah*. You will never find a change in the *sunnatullah*.**" (Quran 35:43)

Let me now underline a universal truth. Though some may find it difficult to comprehend, the truth is the truth!

From the instance the point begins to expand to infinity, everything that has occurred and will occur based on the expanding universe principle, is a known and an immutable constant in the sight of the Creative Power!

The history of man within this grand event is not even worth mentioning!

Doubtlessly there are such innumerous conscious species within the cosmos; it is beyond the comprehension of man! All of it is evaluated within the scope of *sunnatullah*.

The Rasul of Allah (saw) says: "If you had known the things I know, you would laugh less and weep more! You could not rest at ease in your beds; you would escape to the mountains, yelling 'Allah! Allah!'"

What is the Rasul of Allah (saw) trying to say with these words?

If we can READ the *sunnatullah*... We will begin to recognize the primary principles of the Universal Law:

1. **The whole of creation, whether consciously or unconsciously, are fulfilling their absolute servitude by living in compliance with the purpose of their creation!**

"**...The seven heavens** (all creation within the seven dimensions of consciousness) **and the earth** (the bodies) **and whatever is in them** *continue their existence through* **Him** (*tasbih*). **And there is not a thing that does not continue its existence through His** *hamd* (the reality of the Names comprising one's essence [*Rabb*] is the evaluator of this continual existence), **but you do not understand their** [way of, discourse, disposition] **disclosure...**" (Quran 17:44)

"(All) **the creatures in the heavens and the earth, and the angels** (all beings and forces pertaining to the spiritual and material worlds) **prostrate to Allah** (in absolute submission to Allah) **without arrogance** (without their constructed illusory identity, i.e. ego)." (Quran 16:49)

2. **The rebelliousness of the creature named Iblis (Satan) is also the product of his absolute servitude! Hence, the implementing of absolute servitude does not prevent one from expulsion and damnation (deviation)!**

"(Iblis) said: **"My** *Rabb***! Because you have led me astray as the outcome of the Names expressed through me, I will surely make** (disobedience; deeds that veil from the *sunnatullah*) **attractive to them on earth** (their bodily lives) **and mislead them all.**" (Quran 15:39)

3. Allah's attribute of 'Power' is called *'Haaqim'* in the *sunnatullah*. Within the universal system and order called *sunnatullah*, the *Qadir* (Power) attribute of Allah necessitates the strong to defeat the weak. Thus, the One whose name is Allah displays His attribute of 'Power.' 'Impotence' or 'Helplessness' is to perish in the system. Hence, there is no room for evaluations based on human emotions and value judgments in the system. To feel pity or to be pitied does not have any effect on the operations of the system. Those who want to be protected need to take the necessary precautions according to their environment. One who lives by their emotions and human opinions and views will suffer the consequences of their choices!

"**O you who have believed! Protect yourselves** (*nafs*) **and your close ones** (the correspondent of your body in the future) **from the Fire whose fuel is people and stones** (idols and other inanimate objects of worship), **over which are appointed angels, who are powerful, harsh and severe and who do not disobey Allah in what He commands them but do as they are commanded.**" (Quran 66:6)

4. Every individual, in every instance, lives the results of his previous actions, whether they are aware of this or not! This is known as consequence (*jaza*). 'Today' is the result of 'yesterday'; 'tomorrow' we will live the results of 'today'! 'Today' is this moment! 'Tomorrow' is after this moment! He who does an iota worth of good will receive its payoff instantly; he who does an iota worth of harm will also receive its consequence instantly. However, depending on the circuitry of the brain through which it is received, it might take time for it to become apparent. For we do not know which circuitry in the brain is involved in producing the action, what kind of feedback the action gives back to the brain, and when and under

what conditions this feedback will be rendered effective in the brain.

"**The book** [the record of the individual's life] **will be laid open; and those who are guilty will be filled with dread at the information they see and will exclaim: 'Oh, woe unto us! What kind of a book** (recorded information) **is this! It leaves out nothing, small or great, but takes all our thoughts and deeds into account!' They will find in their presence all that they have done! Your *Rabb* does not wrong anyone.**" (Quran 81:49)

"**And when the recorded pages are made public.**" (Quran 81:10)

"**Whoever does an iota worth of good will see it, and whoever does an iota worth of evil will see it.**" (Quran 99:7-8)

5. Every individual will see the results of only the deeds they do. No excuse or compensation is valid in the system for the deed, or the lack thereof, which results in a deprivation of some sort.

"**And man will only accrue the results** (consequences) **of his own labor** (what manifests through him; his thoughts and actions, due to the trigger system)." (Quran 53:39)

6. There is no compensation for the past in the system! Everything that transpires within the system forms a forward motion and no instance is ever relived, hence it is impossible to return to the past. Therefore, there is no compensation for the past! We can only evaluate the present moment. The past is past! There is no recompense for the past (including past *salat*)!

"**Had there been within both** (the heavens [meanings] and the earth [actions]) **gods besides Allah, verily this system would have lost its order.** So exalted (*subhan*) **is Allah,** *Rabb* **of the Throne** (who creates and forms existence from the quantum potential, at will) **beyond the definitions they attribute to Him.**

He is not questioned for what He does, but they will be questioned (they will live the consequences of their action)." (Quran 21:22-23)

7. If one fails to obtain insight in this world, they will forever be blind after the transformation of death!

"**And whoever is blind** (unable to perceive the truth) **in this life** (outer life) **will also be blind in the eternal life to come** (inner life) **and further astray in way** (of thought)." (Quran 17:72)

8. Since the One who is denoted by the name Allah is not a god in the heavens, as some people who are short of knowledge and adequate contemplation think, it is not possible to confront and question this god!

9. Man has the opportunity to attain all that he desires for the afterlife by executing the necessary actions and uploading them to his spirit in this world. After the event of 'changing dimensions' known as death, brain-developing exercises called 'prayer' will have no relevance. With death, the chance of developing the brain will come to an absolute end. Therefore, this world is our only chance to activate the qualities in our brain denoted by the Names of Allah. Whatever the reason or excuse may be, he who fails to use this chance will forever live its consequences!

"So when death finally comes to one of them, he says, 'My *Rabb*, send me back (to worldly life) so that I may do what is necessary for my eternal future** (i.e. live a faithful life which I did not heed or give importance to; the potential that I did not use and activate).' No! (it is impossible to go back!) His words are useless!** (his request is unrecognized in the system) **and behind them is a barrier** (an isthmus, a difference of dimension) **until the Day they are resurrected** (they cannot go back; reincarnation, being reborn for another worldly life is not possible!). **So when the Horn is blown** (when the process of resurrection, i.e. a new beginning commences), **no relationship** (worldly interactions, family relations, titles or familiar faces) **will there be among them that Day, nor will they ask about one another** (in terms of earthly relations)." (Quran 23:99-101)

10. **Every individual existence contains within it the existence subsequent to itself, like the seeds inside a fig or the hidden potential of man inside a drop of sperm. This is true, whether it becomes apparent or not...**

11. **What makes man 'different' is his capacity to ascend within his own heaven or to return to the point of reality within his essence and cleanse himself from his human values and emotions in order to activate the 'caliphate' within!**

"**It is HU who has made you vicegerents upon the earth** (the caliphate attribute is 'made' not 'created'. This fine distinction should be pondered upon with care! A.H.). **Whoever is ungrateful** (whoever denies his vicegerency for the sake of individual values and bodily pleasures) **denies** (the reality) **against his own self! For the disbelief of those who disbelieve the knowledge of reality will not increase anything for them in the sight of their *Rabb* except loss.**" (Quran 35: 39)

12. When a sperm cell makes a leap into a new dimension, nobody feels sorry for the millions of other sperm cells that never make it to the egg and who have to live the consequences of this loss!

Some people think *'sunnatullah'* is different to the *'sunnah* **of the Rasul of Allah'**... But then again, some people think of the Rasul of Allah as a paternal figure! Alas, they have not understood a thing!

The Rasuls are not our fathers or uncles; they are the **Rasuls of Allah**. Sadly, this 'neighbourhood' mentality is still widely in use...

Here is the verse:

"Muhammad is not the father of one of your men! But he is the Rasul of Allah, the final of Nabis (the summit of perfection)." (Quran 33:40)

Hopefully we can quit thinking of him as a father and deservedly evaluate his true essence!

Of course, for someone who labels their imaginary god as **'Allah'** and places Him in the sky and His prophets on earth, *sunnatullah* and the **sunnah of the Rasul** are different things! Even those who read and talk about 'unity' make this fragmentation... Leave those who only see with their external eyes to their own accord...

"Nor does he speak from his own inclinations (imagination)." (Quran 53:3)

This verse alone is sufficient for the thinking brains to discern that the **sunnah of the Rasul and Nabi of Allah** is based upon the *sunnatullah*. I do not feel the need to provide hadith as reference and expand on this topic. Those who wish to may go ahead and do their research.

Every unit of existence, whoever or whatever it may be, is a 'part' that mirrors the 'whole' and manifests His wish through His innate essential qualities (Names).

Those who have not been blessed with the authority to view multiplicity via the point of unity cannot acquire this secret, even if they imitatively accept it...

The one who says the Word of Testimony with full comprehension of its meaning is the one who will enter paradise!

One wonders how many **'humans'** could there possibly be among the seven billion, who would actually **bear witness to the reality** that **'Muhammad is not the prophet of God, but the servant and the Rasul of Allah'** with full awareness and discernment…!

24 June 2005
Raleigh – NC, USA

26

SUNNAT-I RASULULLAH
(The Sunnah of the Rasul of Allah - The Ethics of Allah)

I want to continue the topic of *sunnatullah* in this chapter to ensure it is well understood and to eradicate the illusion 'God is the father, the Rasul is the father' completely. For if we continue viewing these magnificent supremacies with a simplistic approach and treat them akin to the elders of our family the extent of truth from which we will be curtained cannot even be imagined! But no matter what we write and how much we stress the importance of this topic, it is difficult for people to abandon the religious understanding they have constructed in their imagination and to adopt the universal realities that are being revealed to them!

I wonder what I have to do… If I write the things from the past they say "these are things we know". If I write new things they say "we have never heard such things, where are you making this up from?" I just don't know what to do…

But there is one thing I know for sure, and that is our lack of knowledge and understanding of the words **'Allah'** and **'Rasulullah'**… We simply use these words and concepts without ever pondering on what they actually mean!

"The comprehension that you will never comprehend Allah, is the comprehension of Allah" (Abu Bakr)

The Essence of Man

In the same light, we say:

"To comprehend and encompass Muhammad Mustapha (saw), the most profound miracle of the One denoted by the name Allah on earth, will only be the comprehension of our inadequacy to do so!"

For, since we cannot be him, we can never fully understand and decipher what he observed and experienced. Thus, we have no choice but to bow in respect and try our utmost best to comprehend his teachings.

Labels such as 'messenger' denote meanings like 'God's postman,' which imply an inadequate understanding of the **Rasul of Allah** and the One who is indicated by the **name 'Allah'**. Such words reveal illogical assumptions resulting from transgressing one's place.

Muhammad (saw) was a *'Hanif'* in his youth, that is, he refused the concept of godhood, and later, with his *Risalah*, he believed in and advocated only the One denoted by the name Allah, warning people with the universal truth:

"La taj'al maAllahi ilahan akhara fetaq'uda mazmuman mahzula"

"Do not make [up in your mind] **another deity besides Allah** (do not deify your illusory selves)**! Lest you find yourself disgraced and forsaken** (as a result of your *shirq*, dualistic understanding, you will be confined to the limits of your ego rather than manifesting the infinite potential of your essence)**."** (Quran 17:22)

This is because the god concept directs one's attention to the outside world, depriving them from the reality in their own essence, which naturally results in a hellish state of existence.

Sunnatullah necessitates that when one denies someone, they become curtained from everything pertaining to that one, and they will pass on to the next dimension in this veiled state!

Having stressed this point, let us now talk about what it means to comply with the Rasul of Allah...

Some people think I am against the sunnah because I do not believe that complying with the customs and traditions of the idolater Qurayshi community has anything to do with following the sunnah of Rasulullah...

As long as these people do not recognize the qualities and function with which the servant and Rasul of Allah, Muhammad Mustapha (saw), has been created, they will continue their nonsensical judgments, and suffer great disappointment in the end.

The Rasul of Allah (saw) prioritized his life around his primary function as the honored caliphate and did not concern himself with trivial matters related to the way people dressed and lived their daily lives! These things have no significance in respect to the magnificent 'caliphate' attribute offered to man...

It is so sad that while our utmost concern should be to observe the Names of Allah within our essence, getting to know our *Rabb* (essential reality), activating our essential (*Rabbani*) qualities and implementing them into our lives, observing the *sunnatullah* and the infinitely various ways in which it becomes manifest in our perceived universe, we are instead concerned with clothes and beards!

The Rasul of Allah (saw) merely showed his respect to the customs and traditions of the Qurayshi people and thus complied with them; not because they held any significance to him but because he did not want to disrespect his community. What kind of a mentality advocates these customs as the sunnah of **Rasulullah**? If such people cannot break out of their cocoons and attain insight into the actual reality, they will forever be deprived of the perfection of caliphate that **Rasulullah** (saw) wanted people to activate and implement in their eternal lives. Fruitless will be their end...

The Rasul is the Rasul of Allah, and thus, his sunnah is the sunnah of Allah, i.e. *sunnatullah*! He does not have a sunnah of his own, independent from the sunnah of Allah!

"Nor does he speak from his own inclinations (imagination).**"** (Quran 53:3)

This verse is not only in reference to the Quran; its meaning is not limited to the verses that were revealed to him!

Even the topic about which he said **"you know better than me"** was said with the intention to leave people to their own accord as they did not understand what he was saying. It was not possible for the Rasul (saw) to share his knowledge on this topic. For, if he had expounded an unknown mechanism of the *sunnatullah* in regards to this topic, it could have been subject to misunderstanding and resulted in many misinterpretations. Hence, even this incident is a clear indication that **the Rasul of Allah did not intervene with the customs and lifestyle of the Qurayshi community, as long as they did not impede with his primary purpose.**

But when something held value and relevance to the *sunnatullah* he intervened and corrected, like for example when in regards to taking ablution, he warned: **"do not splash the water but wipe your face with it"** so the water can be thoroughly absorbed by the skin cells.

May Allah help us to understand the true function for which the **Rasul of Allah** (saw) has been created and grant us the comprehension that the **Sunnah of the Rasul of Allah**, *is* the **Sunnah of Allah**.

8 July 2005
Raleigh – NC, USA

27

BI-IZNI-HI
(WITH HIS PERMISSION)

The biggest gift the **Rasul of Allah** (saw) has given those who comprehend the **Word of Unity**, and know that its proper application will bring paradise, is the *Basmalah*, or the understanding pertaining to ***B-ismi-Allah-ar-Rahman-ar-Rahim***!

The most elevated life in paradise will be bestowed on those who comprehend the meaning of the *Basmalah*, to the extent their natural disposition allows them.

The reason why **man is the most honored of all creation** is due to his ability to understand and apply the meaning of these words. This honor belongs only to the ***muqarribun*** (those who have attained certainty; *yakeen*) among those who come to this world as the fortunate (*said*) ones.

The *Basmalah* isn't something to be repeated, it is the articulation of an experience! Its due articulation thus belongs to people at this level; the intimates of reality. But we generally repeat this through faith and imitation and expect paradise from our *Rabb* in return!

Another important topic is intercession (*shafaat*). For whom will the Rasul of Allah (saw) intercede, or is interceding? If intercession hasn't reached us in this world, will it have any benefit in the next? Or, how much can one of us help another?

Under what conditions is it possible to take advantage of intercession?

One of the verses in the ***Ayat al-Qursi*** reveals **the ways in which Allah's administration becomes manifest and how much external factors or intercession can alter this administration**:

"*man zallazi yashfa'u indeHU illa Bi-iznihi.*"

"Who can intercede without *Bi-iznihi*." (Quran 2:255)

You may wonder why I translated half the sentence but left the '*Bi-iznihi*' in the original Arabic. This is because this phrase is the pivotal point of the subject.

'*Bi-izni-Hi*'...

As I stated earlier, if we want to decipher the secrets in the Quran we must use the key denoted by the letter 'B'. If the secret of this letter is not ascertained we will always postulate a God somewhere beyond. Unfortunately, although this secret is contained in the original and most of the current translations of the Quran, updated interpretations have overlooked the letter 'B' and its significance.

Whereas...

B-izni-Hi denotes the **unique composition of the Names** comprising the person's essential reality.

In this light, the verse should be translated as:

"Who can intercede without the force that emanates from the dimension of names comprising the reality of your self?"

Indeed, look at how other verses accentuate this reality:

"Except the one to whom the *Rahman* has given permission and accepted his word (the word "*illa* (*only*) *Allah*")." (Quran 20:109)

"*...asta'ighnu Bi-llahi...*"

"...Seek the continual manifestation of the Names of Allah (from your essence in respect of its *Uluhiyyah*; from the forces of the Names comprising your being) **and have patience..."** (Quran 7:128)

"Ya ayyuhallazina amanu Aminu Billahi..."

"O you who have believed; *Aminu B'illahi...*[31]"

That is, "O you who have believed, believe in Allah in accord with the meaning signified by the letter B..." (Quran 4:136)

"Wa minannasi man yakulu amanna Billahi ve Bil yawmil akhiru wa ma hum Bimu'mineen."

And of the people are some who say, "We believe in Allah in accord with the meaning of the letter B (with the belief that the Names of Allah comprise their being) **and the Life after** (that they will forever live the consequences of their deeds)" **but in fact, their faith isn't in line with this reality! (Quran 2:8)**

"Fa aminu Billahi wa Rasulihin Nabiyyul Ummiyyilladhee..."

"So believe in Allah, whose Names comprise the essence of your being, and his Rasul, the Ummi Nabi..." (Quran 7:158)

"Faamma alladheena amanu biAllahi waiAAtasamu bihi fasayudkhiluhum fee rahmatin minhu wafadlin wayahdeehim ilayhi siratan mustaqeema."

"As for those who believe in Allah, the essence of everything, and hold fast unto Him as their essential reality - HU will admit them to grace (*rahmah*) **and bounty** (the awareness of the qualities of the Names) **and guide them to Himself** (enable the observation

---

[31] Among all the worlds that are constituted by the meanings of the names of Allah, your reality, existence, and being also comprise the Names of Allah. Your Rabb, your very Reality is the *al-Asma* (the Names). Therefore, neither you nor anything else around you is anything other than the manifestations of these Names. So do not be of those who fail to see this non-dual reality, and who give a separate existence to things (like God) they believe is 'other' than Allah. Such duality will only result in burning, both in this life and the next. For further information: *Introductory Information To Understanding The Quran*

of their innermost essence) **on a straight path** (*sirat al-mustaqim*).**" (Quran 4:175)

"*Walaw shaa rabbuka laamana man fee alardi kulluhum jamee'an afaanta tukrihu ainnasa hatta yakoonoo mumineena*

Wama kana linafsin an tumina illa biidhni Allahi wayaj'alu alrrijsa 'ala alladheena la ya'qiloona."

"Had your Rabb (the reality of the Names comprising your essence) **willed, all those who live on earth would surely have attained faith, all of them entirely... So then, will you compel the people to become believers?"**

"It is not for a soul to believe unless the unique composition of Allah's Names comprising his essence permits." (Quran 10:99-100)

This is why:

"*Ma'ala arrasooli illa albalaghu*"

"No more is the Rasul bound to do except to provide the knowledge (of the reality and its requisites)..." (Quran 5:99)

"*La ikhraha fidDeen...*"

"There is no compulsion in [acceptance of] **the religion** (the system and order of Allah; *sunnatullah*)**..."** (Quran 2: 256)

This is why intercession, or help, can only be valid if the person's natural disposition suits that particular situation!

The quality of the name *al-Fatir*, which is the former of natural dispositions, takes place within the person's own dimension of Names that comprise the person's *Rabb* (dimension of *Rububiyyah*).

"*Faaqim wajhaka lilddeeni haneefan fitrata Allahi alladhee fatara a'innasa A'alayha la tabdeela likhalqi Allahi dhalika a'iddeenu alqayyimu walakinna akthara a'innasi la ya'lamoona.*"

"Set your face (consciousness) **as a Hanif** (without the concept of a deity-god, without making *shirq* to Allah, i.e. with the consciousness of non-duality) **towards the One Religion** (the only system and order)**, the natural disposition** (*fitrah*) **of Allah** (i.e. the primary system and mechanism of the brain) **upon which Allah has created man. There is no change in the creation of Allah. This is the infinitely valid System** (*deen al-qayyim*) **but most people do not know."** (Quran 30:30)

Here, the holographic reality of today overlaps with what is signified through the phrase 'the part mirrors the whole'.

The manifestation of the attribute of the quantum potential (*Rahmaniyyah*) within the angle projecting from the POINT... *Rahim*, formed by the productivity of this projection, brings about all the various meanings derived from the dimension of Names. This is referred to as the '*Arsh*,' which denotes universal prolificacy – though not in terms of the perceived material world – and '*Qursi*', the actualization and dominance of the reality of the names (*Rububiyyah*)!

Since the part reflects the whole, every individual unit of existence contains the *Rabb*, i.e. the compositions of Names, which express themselves in degrees from the individual's heaven (brain) to their body!

This applies to all units, and hence the holographic reality denotes this system.

My understanding of the Rasul's (saw) words **"The part mirrors the whole"** is this truth.

Though we say the part and the whole, all of it is One reality in the sight of the knowledge of the Divine.

This is revealed by the verses:

"HU created you from ONE single soul – 'I'ness (in the macro plan this is known as the *Reality of Muhammad* and *The First Intellect*, in the micro plan it is known as the human consciousness and *The Grand Intellect*)**."** (Quran 7:189)

"In the afterlife, all of them will come to Him as ONE." (Quran 19:95)

That is, in divine knowledge, there are no parts or division; there is only a SINGLE field. Most people may not find this easy to comprehend.

The whole universe is like a single existence, with all its inner and inter dimensions, or with all its universes within its universes. This has also been referred to as **the Grand Spirit** (*Ruh'ul Azam*).

But will we ever comprehend the qualities and functions of **man** and his creation?

This is what we will look at next…

15 July 2005
Raleigh – NC, US

28

INNER & OUTER DIMENSIONS
(ANFUS AND AFAQ)

In the previous chapter we said:

The manifestation of the attribute of Rahmaniyyah within the angle projecting from the POINT... Rahim, formed by the productivity of this projection, brings about all the various meanings derived from the dimension of Names. This is referred to as the 'Arsh,' which denotes universal prolificacy -though not in terms of the perceived material world- and 'Kursi', the actualization and dominance of Rububiyyah!

Since the part reflects the whole, every individual unit of existence contains the Rabb, i.e. the compositions of Names, which express themselves in degrees from the individual's heaven (brain) to their body!

I want to now approach this topic from another angle:

***Jinni* sourced data** constantly turn man's attention towards the sky, the infinite space, the exterior realms, in order to prevent him from turning towards his essence.

Those who are captivated by such whisperings and are influenced by their incitements prevent others from reading the prayers for protection made of verses from the **Quran** and supplications of the

The Essence of Man

Rasul of Allah. Whereas repeating these prayers on a regular basis will shield and protect one from such influences. **The invisible beings** called the '*jinn*' do not want humans to become conscious of the caliphate secret in their essence. Thus, preventing humans from reaching this reality is their primary mission. I have covered this topic extensively in ***Spirit, Man, Jinn*** and ***Intellect and Faith***. The section **'Why the satanic *jinn* are enemies of Man'** expounds specifically this topic. This is why the *jinn* are known for their satanic attributes.

They direct man's attentions to the outer space to seek his *Rabb*, the Kursi, and the Arsh... As though these are material, tangible phenomenon!

If we want to recognize the structural qualities denoted by the Names of Allah and discern the system and order known as *sunnatullah* without succumbing to such detracting influences...

If we want to truly READ and understand the Quran to decipher the secrets it contains and recognize the immutable system and how it forms what... We must first become cognizant of the following:

If a verse in the Quran is talking about a human or another individual existence, we have to remember the 'mirroring effect' of the part and evaluate the word 'Allah' or the 'Names of Allah' in light of this. That is, as the desired manifestations emerging from the essence of the individual. In other words, as the various levels of unfolding pertaining to the individual's essential reality.

If, on the other hand, the verse is talking about a universal concept, then we have to evaluate the same Names in respect of their levels of expression in the universal dimension!

If we want to discern the attributes of **the One denoted by the name Allah we need to examine the chapter *al-Ikhlas*.**

To comprehend the Absolute Essence (*dhat*) **of Allah is inconceivable, it is impossible!**

The attribute points to the *dhat* but it can never encompass it! As such, it is unreasonable to contemplate the *dhat* of Allah.

Muhammad's (saw) best friend Abu Bakr's (ra) testimony: **"The comprehension that you will never comprehend Allah, is the**

comprehension of Allah" is the articulation of the completion of his ascension!

Indeed, if this reality can be correctly discerned and experienced, one will begin to observe, through insight, the dominion and administration of the *Rabb* upon His servants...

"Sanureehim ayatina fee afaqi wafee anfusihim..."

"We will show them Our signs in the afaq (horizons – outside) **and in the anfus** (inside, within their consciousness)**..."** (Quran 41:53)

"Wafee alardi ayatun lilmuqineena Wafee anfusikum afala tubsiroona."

"And on the earth (the body) are signs for the certain (who observe the qualities of the Names that comprise their being) and **within your own selves** (the essence of the self). **Will you still not see** (discern)?" (Quran 51:20-21)

Hence, in this observation, one will see that whatever is in the outer and the inner, absolute strength and power belongs only to the *RABB*, and that *RABB* is Mureed!

"Innallaha yaf'alu ma Yureed."

"Indeed, Allah does as He wills." (He forms what He wills to manifest from His knowledge with Power; Knowledge – Will – Power) (Quran 22:14)

This verse points to Allah's attribute of will called '***Mureed***'.

"The heart of the servant is between the two fingers of Allah."

Every instance, he takes on a different color with the manifestation of his *Rabb*, the name composition!

"And your *Rabb* has decreed that you serve only Him (He created you to manifest the qualities of His Names)..." (Quran 17:23)

For, the *Rabb* is One, there are no other *Rabb*s.

"Iyyaka na'budu wa iyyaka nasta'een." (Quran 1:5)

External manifestations are a reflection of servitude to the internal qualities of the Names (*Rabb*).

Come, my friend, do not squander your life... **Comprehend well the *sunnatullah* and make the best of the knowledge you have been given. Time wasted can never be compensated, come to your senses, do not misuse your time, do not dissipate your life with nonsense things disguised by Satan as alluring. Rather, prepare yourself with this knowledge for the eternal abode awaiting you after this world.**

Cut your losses while you still can...

22 July 2005
Raleigh, NC – USA

29

DEITY-CENTRIC RELIGION?

Perhaps we need to question the fundamentals of the topic:

A deity centered, or a Muhammad (saw) **centered, understanding of religion?**

Yes, I have indeed thrown yet another controversial ball into the court, but do forgive me; the fine distinction between the two implies enormous significance! In fact, failure to recognize this difference could mean the inability to rid one's self from 'religious savvy' to attain the reality of the Religion!

So what is this important difference?

According to the general conception of **Muslims**, religion is a **deity-centered belief system**. That is, even though Muslims always say Allah is 'everywhere' or 'free from location', nevertheless this 'deity-god' whom they have named **'Allah'** is always conceived as being somewhere in the heavens or in the upper dimensions of space somewhere! Hence, they believe in a god who is somewhere *beyond*. But this is a misconceived sense of duality, an apparent *shirq*; an act of associating partners to Allah! Almost all people with such dualistic concepts believe in a postulated god, whom they label 'God' or 'Allah', and whom they construct based on their own culture, environment and imagination.

Some people, based on their own nonsensical reasons, forbid the contemplation on the verses in the **Quran** in relation to this topic, and hence their **'personal god'** becomes fixated in their brain, leaving no room for progress or development!

According to their assumptions and misconceptions, this personal god, picks a prophet for itself from among the earthlings, and recruits him as its postman-delivery man-messenger on earth! And all of this happens by way of a messenger angel it 'sends' down to earth!

Let's digress from the subject for an instant: Those who believe in UFOs and extraterrestrial beings claim these angels, or what people have come to accept as gods, are an advanced race from space.

Indeed, beings from space may have come, and they may still do so! Denying this possibility altogether would be nonsensical. **However, to think these beings are angels or gods is an unacceptable mistake! The teachings of the Rasul of Allah (saw) attach no relevance to such things**; we must understand this well.

The **Antichrist** (*Dajjal*) who will claim to be a god visiting his servants on earth will also use this **deity-centered religious** approach to subjugate those who believe in a deity-god to submit to him! Only a handful of people on earth will actually refuse him!

The **'Messiah'** awaited by the Jews and Christians isn't actually Jesus (as); it is the *Dajjal*! **Jesus (as)** is to **emerge after the *Dajjal*** comes to claim he is god. The *Dajjal* is going to be exterminated by Jesus (as) in person, who is going to emerge on earth at the age of 33. Then he is going to spend 7 to 11 years with the *Mahdi*, the final Reviver on earth, before the **Agog and Magog** race from North Asia invade the Middle East. After this period, **Jesus** (as) will live until he is 73 – a total of 40 years on earth. All of this is based on the various hadith of the **Rasul of Allah** (saw). Further information can be found in *The Mystery of Man* under the section **'The Signs of Doomsday'**.

Going back to our main topic, **'a deity-based religion'** is essentially a materialistic one.

According to a **deity-based religious** view, the Quran and hadith have only literal meaning and value.

A **deity-based religious** view dictates that God literally has a hand!

A **deity-based religious** view claims God has a double pan balance scale (apparently God hasn't yet discovered the digital and other advanced versions!).

This kind of religious understanding does not encourage contemplation, it doesn't think to realize all of this metaphoric language could actually be used to denote certain realities to man...

As such, everything in a **deity-based religious** view is based on the material world. There is no room for questioning, pondering, contemplating or even thinking! There are only commands and their blind applications!

Under the name 'Comparative Fiqh' certain allegorical verses have been construed according to the current time and age and accepted within the scope of religion and shariah (Islamic law). Hence, the construal of Quranic verses based on that particular time and age are now taken as though they are the laws of religion.

According to a **deity-centered religion** *salat* and fasting are like debts that must be paid to god. If you fail to do so, god will send you to prison, or rather to hell!

A deity-centered religious view says: "We only obey the commands and do not think about the rest. He knows better what is what; we do not need to know anything else. If there were a need, He would have let us know. Our duty is only to obey His orders and do our worship. It is not our place to question the wisdom and the reason and ponder on the rest..."

The other very clichéd phrase of this view is: "We're all going to die and everything is going to become apparent on Doomsday!"

As for the **religious view centered on Muhammad** (saw) **the Rasul of Allah and the final Nabi**... Far from a materialistic approach, this is the view endorsed by all of the intimates of reality, the Sufi masters, **from Haji Bektashi Wali and Imam Ghazali to Abdulqadir Jilani and Sheikh Bahaaddin Naqshibandi**, who when told "you seem arrogant" replied "this isn't arrogance (*kibr*), it is magnificence (*kibria*)"... And many, many others...

Muhammad (saw) was a ***Hanif***. He knew well the invalidity of the deity-god concept, and at the age of 39, he declared to his idolater community **"there is no god or godhood, there is only Allah (*La ilaha illaAllah*)."**

The most important point here is to recognize what 'Allah' references. **When duly researched and examined it becomes clear that Allah is not a reference to a deity-god to be comprehended far beyond, but rather that Allah is the force, the power and presence within the essence of every unit of existence, of everything! Instead of turning to exterior and outer dimensions, individuals can attain that force and power by turning inner to the depths of their own essence, at which point they will realize their individual nonexistence and declare unity: "Only Allah exists!"**

Hence, there are no angels descending from the skies but forces in the form of knowledge **(Gabriel)** emerging from one's essence to his consciousness. Because the brain constantly creates forms for the raw data it receives to its database with its *'Musawwir'* quality and outputs this to the consciousness, people perceive angels in forms.

The Rasul of Allah (saw) articulated the reality of the One whose name is Allah within his own essence. *Risalah* is the manifestation through revelation (*wahy*) of the attribute of Knowledge pertaining to this reality.

It goes **from the inner to the outer**, from the essence to the exterior, not the other way around and most definitely not from the skies down to the flesh-bone body on earth!

When this knowledge of reality becomes manifest in the form of disclosing the ***sunnatullah***, the immutable constants of Allah's system, in order to enable people to **READ** and apply the necessary practices of the system, it is called ***Nubuwwah***.

Allah, in respect of his Absolute Essence (*dhat*) is an Absolute Unknown (*ghayb*) to us. We can only know Him to the extent of Rasulullah's (saw) disclosure.

Our knowledge of Allah is not derived from our own illusion and imagination but from the teachings of the **Rasul of Allah** (saw), from what he has revealed to us through the Quran and hadith. We contemplate on the reference of Allah based on this knowledge but never condition and confine Him to our understanding!

Rasulullah-centered religion is the name of the system and order comprising the infinite dimensions and universes within universes! Islam is the name of the system in which the products of ONE knowledge and power reside in absolute submission within the infinite dimensions of existence.

"In the sight of Allah, Islam is the religion" is an expression of this truth.

Therefore, **Rasulullah**-centered understanding is the Religion, but a deity-centered one is only religious savvy.

The other important aspect of the **Rasulullah-centered approach** is about **vicegerency**. All units of existence are manifestations reflecting the Names and Attributes of Allah, based on the holographic reality and hadith **'the part mirrors the whole.'**

The best way to discern this is to align our thoughts such that it goes from the one towards the many (from the whole to the part)!

Once this is achieved, we will realize that all the Names and Attributes belonging to what Allah references are the forces and qualities inherent in every single person and unit of existence. Furthermore, we will know that 'angels' are the forces comprising the degrees of the manifestation of these qualities, emerging from the essence of man to the database of his consciousness...

Aleem, Mumeet and *Haseeb*, **manifest** as Gabriel, Azrael **(the transformer)** and Munkar-Nakir **(the accountants)** respectively!

There are no inanimate and unconscious beings in the Rasulullah-centered understanding! For every unit of existence subsists with the qualities of the Names of Allah.

Man is the only existence among all living things on earth to feel 'sympathy and mercy' and the capacity to observe the magnificent *sunnatullah* of Allah! Hence, he is the most honored among creation (*ashraf-i mahluq*)!

"One without sympathy deserves no sympathy"!

Rasulullah's (saw) words in reference to vermin: "Kill all things that are harmful!" need to be comprehended and evaluated well.

Everyone who respects the lives of others has the right to live in the **Rasulullah**-centered conception of religion.

According to this view, every unit of existence is facilitated by its *Rabb* (the unique composition of Names comprising its essence) to fulfil the purpose of its creation. This may be both towards a favorable end or an unfavorable one. This is the display of absolute servitude.

In the **Rasulullah-centered religion**, all spiritual practices in the form of prayer, *dhikr*, *salat* and fasting etc. are done with the intention of actualizing the forces and qualities pertaining to one's *Rabb* within one's own essence rather than to please a deity-god. **The phrases "for the pleasure of Allah" or "to please Allah" entail the suitability or compatibility of a situation to one's optimal essential reality.** For as a result of this, one is able to manifest a quality of his ideal essential self!

"**And man will only accrue the results** (consequences) **of his own labor** (what manifests through him; his thoughts and actions, due to the trigger system)." (Quran 53:39)

This verse is clear enough for thinking brains to comprehend the reality!

In short, **a deity-god centered religion** is directed towards an external God.

Whereas religion centered around the **Rasul of Allah, Muhammad** (saw), is for 'humans' **who begin with faith in Allah (as disclosed by the Rasul of Allah)** and then discover the various degrees of divinity and the forces and perfect qualities pertaining to them, all within their own essence.

29 July 2005
Raleigh, NC – USA

30

KNOWLEDGE – WILL – POWER

We cross the Bridge of *Siraat* with the three horsemen of Doomsday, and the additional help of other forces:

Knowledge, Will and Power!

Aleem, Mureed, Qadir!

Everything that transpires from our brain is due to the respective expressions of these qualities.

Knowledge refers to the brain's database…

Will denotes the person's capacity to apply, or zeal…

And **Power** is the energy that converts what is willed into action!

At every instance of our lives these three forces are at work… Just as they are present and active within every single one of us, they are also actively functional in the same way in every animate being in the universe!

For the **name Allah references** the creator of us and everything in the universe, who knows His infinite qualities with His *Aleem* name, who wills to see these qualities through His *Mureed* name, and who observes them with the **power** denoted by His *Qadir* name.

This is the mechanism at work throughout everything in the world; this is how these qualities become manifest through individual beings...

There is an individual consciousness within the brain, or the memory of every unit of existence, formed by the synthesis of all the data received until that point. This applies not only to humans but to animals and beings that may not be visible to us. This is the manifestation of **Knowledge**.

This database naturally wants to output the data it contains, as this is how a database functions! This 'want' is referred to as **'Will'** (*Mureed*) and it is formed in the brain automatically. We refer to the part we actually pick up on as "what comes to mind"...

Ultimately, when the strength of this will exceeds a particular threshold, it begins to actualize, which is rendered possible by the potential and amount of energy denoted by 'Power' (*Qadir*).

This circulation of Knowledge-Will-Power is formed simultaneously in the brain and is in full circulation at all times.

"Every day HU manifests Himself in yet another way." (Quran 55:29)

'Hu' isn't something in space, **Hu is the reality of your essence! Hu is the totality of this universal structure; Hu is the Absolute Universal One!**

There are infinite activities of the Knowledge-Will-Power relation in the brain, but only a few of them are disclosed to our consciousness. When we become conscious of something, even if we don't speak this thought, its presence in our consciousness means it has been output, which is then re-admitted to the brain's database as feedback, and re-processed for another output.

This is a fixed system. It does not change.

"...Whatever is in the heavens and the earth belongs to Allah (to manifest His Names)**... Whether you show what is within your consciousness** (your thoughts) **or conceal it, Allah will bring you to account for it with the quality of the Name *al-Hasib*."** (Quran 2:284)

No excuse is valid in this mechanism!

Anything you output is either due to data you stored in your database or **received genetically**. In any case, it is the output of something within you!

The proverb "The gods visit the sins of the fathers upon the children" refers to this reality.

The **'Knowledge-Will-Power'** mechanism, though infinite in respect of the whole, is expressed in every iota of existence according to the capacity and natural disposition (fate) of the individual.

Prayers and curses are also products of the same mechanism of the brain based on one's database.

Every individual's experience derives from itself. Hence, every experience is a unique one!

Every unit evaluates another through its own perception. Thus, its ability to perceive another is limited by its own perceptive capacity.

Rasulullah (saw) says: **"Do not curse anyone. For, if the curse is not their due, it will come back and strike you!"**

That is, if according to **your perception** someone deserves to be cursed for some reason, but in reality that person is innocent or a victim of that situation, i.e. the person does not actually deserve to be cursed, then the curse will not reach the person, it will rebound from their protective shield and return with the same speed and afflict the curser instead!

Are the things we perceive as **'right'** or **'wrong'**, according to the judgments based on our database, actually congruent with how they are perceived by the system…?

When we find ourselves in a situation, our first reaction should be: "I wonder what I have done wrong to be in this situation" rather than blaming others!

For the verse says: **"And whatever strikes you of disaster, it is the result of what your hands have earned."** (Quran 42:30) **'What your hands have earned' is a reference to the database of one's brain.**

Indeed, he who deserves will find what he deserves. And if he does not deserve it then it will find the doer!

Anyway, without digressing further, let me drive my point home:

Prayer or *salat* (turning towards one's essence) is either a request that is made from an exterior God, or **it is the process of actualizing one's wishes through using the forces and potentials within one's essence in congruence with the information contained within the database.**

In short, when someone prays, they 'will' to manifest certain qualities (knowledge) pertaining to Allah comprising their essence, and does so in accord with their power. This is true whether they are a learned, knowledgeable man, or whether they are completely ignorant!

"**Seek the continual manifestation of the Names of Allah** (from your essence in respect of its *Uluhiyyah*; from the forces of the Names comprising your being)…" (Quran 7:128)

Knowledge-Will-Power is an intrinsic mechanism inherent in the human structure!

Praying to and seeking things from god(s) outside is nothing but pure ignorance and unawareness. For anything that you acquire is **from yourself, from your own** qualities! It is the output or expression of the qualities and attributes pertaining to the One denoted by Allah that become manifest through **you**!

I recommend reading *A Guide to Prayer and Dhikr* in this light and with this consciousness!

5 August 2005
Raleigh – NC, USA

31

HOW CAN YOU CALL IT A LIE?

He has no idea about his own body let alone the universe!

He walks around with a tough guy attitude, giving orders to everyone, but his consciousness dwells at the level of **a rural village**, despite the fact that his body may be living in London, Paris, Istanbul or New York!

As **his brain is blocked with the conditionings and value judgments he received as a kid from his jerkwater town life**, he still views the world from the narrow window of his tiny **village-like, 'local' mentality**!

His label says he's a **'great man'**! His label cons people into thinking he has a lot of knowledge! But in reality, he lives in his world with the things he learnt and memorized in his rural community, oblivious of his **'villager label'**!

Is this bad? Is it a sin? Is it forbidden?

No… Not at all!

The only thing is, due to his lack of awareness of this situation, he will not be able to surpass his identity; he will inevitably waste his life and consume himself with worthless things! And thus, inadvertently, he will also drag others like himself into erroneous ways!

He may be a genius in physics, medicine, chemistry or astronomy, but he still dwells in **his little rural village**. He approaches people, events and life with the values he acquired and fosters in **his *rustic* mind**.

He has learnt religion from a course taught by villagers. This education laid the foundations in his brain and initialized the direction of his thoughts!

Even if he has become a professor in his later life, because **his brain is blocked with judgments based on inadequate data acquired during his younger years**, he is never able to overcome these thought patterns!

Due to being raised in a system that dictated memorization and prohibited questioning and research, he anxiously refrains from synthesizing the information he acquires to produce new outcomes as if it would lead him to danger!

Where does earth stand in respect of the universal realities? How much of the billions and billions of activities going on in his body does he have insight into?

What is his brain, how does it work? What exactly is this being he calls '**me**' or '**I**'? He refrains from giving the slightest thought to such topics… they scare him!

Perhaps he has memorized a one liner such as "**everything is god, everything is a part of god, god is me, I am!**"

And? What next? What has memorizing this brought him? How does this contribute to his life? What kind of comfort does this awareness offer him?

If knowing this leads him to live an irresponsible corporeal life, then it has obviously defeated the purpose since that is how all animals live their lives already! What kind of a 'difference' has this awareness given him? What has he gained? Which doors of mystery have opened up to him with this knowledge, what sort of new secrets has it helped him acquire and experience and enrich his life with?

What kind of **'enlightenment'** is this if he has no idea of the *sunnatullah*? In fact, he is not even aware of it!

The expense of deceiving one's self is the biggest expense in life!

They say "but he knows the Quran!"

Why? What for?

He claims he is the **'Reality'** and the **'One'** but does he actually know what the **QURAN** is?

Please don't say: **"It is the book sent down by God to his prophet!"**

The **Quran** says:

"***Rahman*** (*the absolute possessor of all the qualities denoted by the Names*), ***taught the Quran*** (*formed the structural qualities pertaining to the dimension of Names*), ***created MAN, and taught him eloquence*** (*manifested the qualities of the Names on man*)." (Quran 55:4)

How was man created? After which stage?

When man was inexistent, to whom was the **Quran** taught?

What does it mean to **'teach'** the Quran? Why does the **Quran** expound these things to us?

As a reaction to **Darwin**'s theory that man is an advanced species of ape, the view of **Intelligent Design** started to gain popularity in the United States. According to this view, man was created by a **Creative Intelligence** independent of the apes...

Fa tabarak Allahu ahsanal Halikeen!

The Sufi saints talked about **The First Intellect** (*aql-i Awwal*) over a thousand years ago, as **the manifestation of Allah's attribute of knowledge from the essence of the universe...**

They said the **First Intellect**, or Universal Intelligence in today's terminology, **is involved in every movement of every form of existence within the universe...**

Hasn't anybody noticed this?

When some scientist talks about **Creative Intelligence** and **Intelligent Design** the whole world is shaken up! Whereas this is merely another way of expressing the meaning of **Allah's *al-Fatir* name**: **designing, planning, ordering, timing, administrating,** and so on... All of these are synonymous with **creating**, which is what is implied by the word *'fitrah'* or ***Fatir***!

Many scientists declared: "There is no God" and the intellectuals inclined towards this view, but nobody told them about what **Allah** references, nobody shared the reality expounded by the **Rasul of Allah** (saw)!

Is this how blind and blocked we have become?

Atheism, or rejecting God/godhood, which was presented as the view of modern science, was advocated first by **Abraham (as)** (first as a *Hanif*, then **as the Rasul of Allah**) and then by all of the **Rasuls, Nabis, saints and the seekers of reality of the past**, centuries ago! These eminent people had already declared *"La ilaha"* **(There is no God)** thousands of years ago! They had already established the truth **"There is no God/godhood, there is only Allah"** right at the onset!

"Set your face (consciousness) **as a *Hanif*** (without the concept of a deity-god, without making *shirq* to Allah, i.e. with the consciousness of non-duality) **towards the One Religion** (the only system and order)**, the natural disposition** (*fitrah*) **of Allah** (i.e. the primary system and mechanism of the brain) **upon which Allah has created man. There is no change in the creation of Allah. This is the infinitely valid System** (*deen al-qayyim*) **but most people do not know."** (Quran 30:30)

Rahman **taught the Quran!** This teaching, based on a specific system and order, formed the universes within universes!

The **'Quran'** here, is a general reference to **the Absolute Essence's** (*dhat*) **descension to the world of Names and Attributes** (multiplicity) **to form everything that is perceived and not perceived; the** *jinni* (all invisible beings) and humans.

Every iota within the cosmos at every instance manifests the knowledge of Allah in different guises, through which the attribute of will transforms into power to create every single unit of existence!

Although the genetic code of an ape is very similar to humans, the advanced apes, whether we call it mutation or an angelic effect, ultimately the divine **knowledge has formed on earth a species from nothing** called 'man.'

In fact, **'declaration'** was the driver of this formation.

'Declaration' is the name of the **operating system** running one's existence program!

The **teaching of the declaration** means creating man with the same operating system running the universe, which is the natural result of *sunnatullah*!

That is, the program that is operating at the macro level is applied at the micro level!

This is why it was said **'the part reflects the whole'**!

This is why the universe has been defined as macro and man as micro.

And this is why many years ago I had said **"Our brain is our micro-cosmos"**.

Just as the universes, with all their dimensional depths, are the manifestations of Allah's names and attributes at various levels and as various compositions, in the same way, man, who has been formed with a program (taught-*talim*) is a micro-world that contains all of these manifestations within himself.

Hadhrat Ali (ra) alluded to this truth 1,400 years ago with his words: **"You think you are a small world, whereas you are a world that is great"**!

Unfortunately, because everything was expressed via metaphors and symbols, the truth has always remained concealed.

"Man is the twin brother of the Quran" also refers to the same truth.

The concept referenced by the word Quran in *"**Rahman** taught **the Quran**"* is not the same concept we gather from the 'holy book' we hold in our hands today.

The Essence of Man

The **Quran** in this verse is a reference to the code of the primary operating system with which Allah created the cosmos, or the **Primary Book**. Since man also exists with the same system he has been defined as the twin brother or the micro of the macro universe and has been referenced synonymously with the Book revealed to him. The **Quran** being 'revealed' to the **Rasul of Allah** (saw) means he was able to **READ** (*iqra*) the universal system. Hence, it is said "The **Quran** was **revealed** at once."

As this knowledge was imparted to the people, the **Quran** as we know it was formed. **The Quran is knowledge!** It is not paper, leather or a collection of pages!

If man can cleanse himself from imitation, subconscious information in the form of memorized and conditioned data, and begin to question his essence and evaluate the knowledge he acquires in this way, the path to becoming **'moralized with the morals of Allah'** will open to him. He will begin to **READ** the *sunnatullah*! He will become the eyes with which He sees, the ears with which He hears and the speech through which He speaks! But the people won't recognize **Him**! Just as they didn't recognize the **Rasul of Allah** (saw) and told him: **"you stroll through the bazaar and the market place just like one of us"**…

The dualists can only perceive **'Muhammad the orphan'**, they are blind to 'Muhammad, the **Rasul of Allah** (saw)'!

This is such a bounty that only the *intimates of the reality* can confirm and witness its true value!

"So which of the favors of your *Rabb* (the Names comprising your essence – your consciousness and body) **will you deny?"** (Quran 55:13)

Hence, at this level of consciousness, this is how the **Quran** should be **READ**!

Spawned by **atheism**, Darwinism is thought to be the beginning of modern science. Having knocked down the concept of god, it naturally infused the question **"OK then, what is the creative intelligence behind this system and order in the universe?"**

The classic religious/God approach was not able to provide an adequate answer and so ultimately the view based on 'intelligent design' was reached. The thinking brains, despite refusing the concept of a deity-god, were in search of a **'universal creative intelligence' in light of the latest scientific developments**.

Western scientists who were up to date with all of the latest scientific advancements knew there couldn't be a deity dwelling somewhere in space who sent down some heavenly religion, due to this they accepted atheism. However, this wasn't sufficient to shed light on the universal realities they were seeking either, so the motive was to search for the **'Universal Creative Intelligence'**.

This view is the door to Allah, as disclosed by **Muhammad (saw) the Rasul of Allah!**

Many people are now **seeking the reality of the religion of Islam**, beyond the views of the titular Muslims. When this search enables the seekers to recognize *al-Fatir*, they are going to **discover and accept the One referenced by Allah, who's Absolute Essence is an Absolute Unknown**! According to my understanding, this is the outcome of the *Mujaddid*'s **(Reviver)** years of service on earth.

It is impossible for those who become cognizant of the reality at this level to remain as atheists!

May the door to reality be a blessing upon **everyone** who recognizes it!

This is another expression of **'being guided by Allah'** or perceiving and evaluating the reality!

12 August 2005
Raleigh – NC, USA

32

BRAIN BLOCKAGE

This is the biggest issue!

To lock one's self and become blocked and stuck!

"I can't understand… I read and I read but I just don't seem to get it! Just as I think I have it, I realize I haven't understood anything!"

I hear this kind of confession a lot…

Why does this happen?

Because somewhere in the past, perhaps with a very simple command, we have locked our brain, and we are not even aware of it!

We must know with certainty that whatever we may think we are doing to others we are doing to ourselves, and inevitably living the consequences of our own actions!

"Everyone will reap what they sow!"

A simple judgment we may have made in the past during our youth or even during childhood such as "This is what this is about" or "This is only this much" becomes programmed in our brain and we become fixed with that data. **Whenever contrary information is encountered, the brain oversees or ignores it as it has already** fixated itself with the current value. This could be about a book, a person or a religious or social topic, it does not matter!

The brain functions based on the ***sunnatullah*** (the universal mechanics of the system)!

This is why whoever has denied someone or something has blocked themselves in regards to that thing and there is no easy way of turning back!

Can you not erase and restore this information at all?

Of course, the door to repentance is open.

If a person genuinely realizes the wrong they have done and re-evaluates the topic with the sincere intention of correcting it, certain exercises can enable that particular area of the brain to become receptive again to re-questioning and researching the topic in order to unblock and update its database. But this depends on how certain the person becomes of their wrongdoing. Otherwise, the brain will retain the data it has obtained from the past until the person dies, in which case the person will leave this world without having perceived the reality.

One must be completely open to all new things to start with...

One must be a questioner, a searcher; one must never condition and restrict one's self with the existing database!

One must always ask one's self: "**This is what was understood in regards to this topic in the past, I wonder if it can be viewed in a different way today...**" and re-evaluate every new idea and event one encounters in this light... This is the measure that must be taken to avoid the brain from becoming blocked, fixated and stuck.

The majority of people allow their brains to become locked very early in their lives, and unfortunately they spend their adult years shut off to new ideas. Environmental conditioning is the biggest impediment to the brain!

The brain starts getting fixed in regards to many topics at a very early age!

If, for instance, you believed for some reason that a particular thing does not exist, then even if that thing is in front of your eyes you will not see it; you will become blind to it.

This brain-blockage in individuals can also lead to blockage and blindness in communities where the whole community can become fixed and locked in regards to certain topics.

Though the veil in front of the unseen and the unknown is often the source of our blockage, sometimes it can also be due to those who are aware of our blockages taking advantage of these veils.

This is why **"saints are hidden under the veil of Allah"**. That is, our presumptions about **saints and sainthood** block us from recognizing them even if we actually see them. For **our brains have become fixed with a value** we have stored in the past. The only way we can recognize and accept it is if it appears to us as what we have stored it to be!

"They have hearts (consciousness) **with which they cannot understand** (the reality) **they have eyes with which they cannot evaluate what they see, they have ears with which they cannot understand what they hear! They are like livestock** (*an'am*, domestic animals)**, they are even less conscious of the right way: it is they, they who are the** [truly] **heedless!"** (Quran 7:179)

"Allah has set a seal upon their brain's perception of reality; their insight is veiled." (Quran 2:7)

The expression here that **Allah has 'sealed'** their perception is a reference to the **blindness and blockage** that forms in the person as this is how *sunnatullah* or the mechanics of the brain's system works! **When one makes a wrong judgment and stores this in their brain even if they encounter the naked truth will not recognize it!**

Denial (*kufur*) **is the coveting of truth**; it is the inability to perceive, and hence the denial of reality, which is again related to blocking the brain. A **denier** (*kafir*) is one who has fixated **(covered)** their brain with other data and thus has become unable to perceive and evaluate Allah, **the Rasul of Allah**, and the **Quran**.

Someone who is not familiar with my work, or hasn't really read it, may deduce from all this that I am referring to an external god in space who literally seals and locks the hearts and minds of people. Whereas, those who READ my work will know and recognize that I am referring to the natural function of the Names of Allah comprising the essential reality of each individual. This is referred to as the administration of Allah in the Quran.

We hold in our hand an important key to understanding the Quran…

The first rule to READ is to abandon all accumulated knowledge from the past and not let them interfere in the evaluation of the new data so it can be perceived in an objective unbiased way.

The second step is to notice the examples, metaphors and allegories that are employed in the data one is reading or perceiving.

Thirdly, to never say: "I already know this, I had heard or read this before" and not have prejudice or prejudgments.

If one happens not to comprehend the topic, they should never deny or refuse the idea, but leave its evaluation and comprehension to time, without hastening to draw any conclusions. For this occurs when either one's database is inadequate, or the person has already formed a judgment regarding this topic at an earlier time, and hence their brain is blocked to new data. In this case, the best thing one can do is remain open to all aspects of the topic as much as they can.

Let us know that most of the judgments we make deprive us from acquiring innumerous secrets pertaining to infinite universal realities.

The cocoon that forms our world of thoughts often becomes our prison rather than the means to emancipate us to infinite new dimensions!

Everything in the universe and in our world is being renewed at every instance!

"**Every instance HU** (the Absolute Essence of Existence) **manifests Himself in yet another way.**" (Quran 55:29)

This verse calls our attention to the universal renewal that is taking place at all times!

Yet we are still awaiting a *Mujaddid* (**Reviver**) to arrive swinging a sword on a horse with an army to call people to a lifestyle of centuries ago!

I probably won't be here to see him, but if you do, know with certainty that the *Mahdi* **Rasul** is not going to call the people and the religious understanding backward to old ways, nor is he going to repeat the conception of the past! On the contrary, he is going to be an **innovator**, a reviver and, as **Rumi** says, he is going to **"talk of new things today"**!

Blocked brains, or like me, those who are living the last period of their life will not see **this blessed person**, but at least we know he is a **REVIVER**! According to **my understanding, he has already come to earth to renew and revitalize our understanding of religion!** Blessed are those who are open to this!

Those who live to see it will send me their blessings!

Whatever you do, try to cleanse your brains from fixated conditionings and blockages lest you be deprived of the universal realities called '*sunnatullah*'!

18 August 2005
Raleigh – NC, USA

33

BI-RABBIHIM

I want to talk a little more about the implications of the letter **B** in the **Quran** and **explore the meaning** of *Bi-Rabbihim* with this **key**. I believe the better this topic is understood, the better some of the **subtleties of the Quran** can be recognized and comprehended.

Bi-Rabbihim points to the unique composition of Names within every individual and its manifestation, which comprises the dimension of *Rububiyyah*.

Bi-Rabbi-Ka points to the composition of Names within **you** that manifest to form the dimension of *Rububiyyah* in **your essence.**

While *Rabbihim* means their *Rabb* or the *Rabb* of the worlds, *Bi-Rabbihim* refers to the force of *Rububiyyah* present within their essential reality that administers on every level from that point.

This does not in any way imply multiple *Rabb*s!

Just like every lamp receives the same electricity from one source, there is only one current or force pertaining to the dimension of *Rububiyyah*. However, each different lamp, or their filaments, is like the different compositions of Allah's Names. You can obtain more information on this in *Revelations*, a book I wrote in 1967.

Let's take a look at one of the verses in the Quran as an example, from chapter *al-Qadr*:

"The angels (**the angelic forces within – wings denote the 2-3-4 dimensions of these forces**) and the Spirit (**the meaning of 'HU' comprising the essence of your existence**) becomes revealed in one's consciousness with the permission (**capacity**) of his *Rabb* (**the composition of Allah's Names comprising his essence**); such that he experiences his inexistence **while experiencing the absolute existence of Allah**, in a state of certainty (*yakeen*) free from all judgments!" (Quran 97:4)

As much as 'Spirit' denotes the afterlife body of the person, its actual reference in the Quran is to the 'connotation' of a thing. That is, when we say 'the spirit of man' we mean 'the general meaning of the name composition comprising the existence of man'. As a matter of fact, to say 'I know your spirit/soul' is a popular usage among people to mean they know each other very well.

What is *Qadr*? How does it descend from the skies? This I want to talk about in the next chapter. But right now, I think we should consider again what the following might mean:

"**There is no animate creature but that He holds its forehead** (the brain; the very qualities of the Names of Allah!)." (Quran 11:56)

"*La ḥawla wa la quwwata illa billah*": There is no initiative or capability except from Allah…

Why is this *dhikr* so important; what can we gain from repeating this phrase?

According to my understanding, the pronoun '*Bi-Rabbihim*' in the Quran, always refers to the Name composition comprising the reality of every individual's existence. This topic has been explored in depth in ***The Mystery of Man***, written in 1985, under the chapters '**Rabb**' and '**Rububiyyah**'. The expression '*Rabb* **of the worlds**' refers to the universal dimension of *Rububiyyah* from which every unique Name composition obtains its force of life at the level of atoms.

Hence, when the letter B precedes a particular word, it adds a significant meaning to it.

Another important note is the word **B-illahi**. The elderly would always prohibit us from giving an oath in the name of Allah using the word '*B-illahi*'. Has anyone wondered why?

Because the word *B-illahi* actually means: **"I hereby talk on behalf of the Allah in my existence"**!

Can we imagine the implications of such a serious statement? Are we even aware of this meaning when we so readily and easily give an oath using the word *B-illahi*?

As can be seen, all of this point to the same reality: There is no God out there to whom we should turn; **we need to turn to the forces pertaining to the Names of Allah in our essence and activate them!** This is what prayer is all about!

If we assume the existence of a god besides the **Names of Allah comprising our essence**, we will be engaging in *shirq* (duality)!

If we seek help, or intercession(*shafaat*) from each other or from the Rasul of Allah (saw) or from other spiritual leaders with the consciousness that these people are also 'servants' who have been successful in activating their intrinsic forces that we couldn't, this won't be considered *shirq*. But if we do this with the assumption that there is an external god beyond and deny our own reality, if we see ourselves as a creation and an external god as the creator, this will be *shirq*.

The important thing is to know your self, be aware of your capacity and incapacity, and to seek help accordingly, without **deifying!**

Whatever it means to seek help from someone regarding worldly matters, it means the same thing to seek help regarding spiritual matters!

Nevertheless, one should also be aware that any help one receives can only be as effective as their essential name composition allows; the natural disposition is not subject to change.

External help will not change our natural skills and capacity, but it can help us realize and actualize them! **This is what '*illa Bi-izni-h*" refers to in the *Ayat al-Qursi*.**

The Essence of Man

As long as we engage in prayer and *dhikr* and continue aspiring our capacity will enhace, as soon as we stop it will go back to its previous state. This is also known as **'*himmah*'** (aspiration). One's *himmah* should be continually active in order for one's capacity to become enhanced and his wishes to be fulfilled accordingly.

If you seek help from the **Rasul of Allah** (saw) or another person who has the capacity to help you but they don't, do not let yourself think or feel differently about that person, look for the answer within yourself, **within your own capacity and natural disposition (*fitrah*)**.

Your Name composition, referenced by the expression '*Bi-Rabbihim*', is absolutely unique. This is why nobody can be an ideal example for anybody, and no one can know their *Rabb* through someone else's path.

Another manifestation of **Hadhrat Ali** (ra) will never come to this world. If one prays to be like him, their prayer will not be accepted. The same reflection will not form twice in the manifest world!

One must know their boundaries when wanting!

Do not try to be like anyone, as this is not possible! Use the full potential of your knowledge to **be yourself!**

It is important to understand the topic of natural disposition well.

Everyone has a unique natural disposition and it is not subject to change. This is the exclusive programming we receive during birth; a unique composition of Allah's names that are coded into our brain. This is why personality traits persist throughout one's lifetime.

Let's imagine that personalities are like jugs of lemonade. Some jugs are filled with delicious and sweet lemonade, whereas others are bitter and tasteless. Astrological influences are like the hands that tilt and shake the jugs, pouring out and revealing the true nature of their contents.

This shouldn't catch you by surprise!

Whatever exists in our perceived world, from the most beautiful to the most awkward, are all created with the **Names of Allah.**

Heaven is heaven compared to hell, and hell is only hell in comparison to heaven!

Hell is like heaven for the demons of hell, and for the dorbeetle living in fecal matter feels like paradise!

Everything is relative! All things are either relatively favorable or relatively unfavorable! What one finds pleasant can seem revolting to another!

Hence, when we feel drawn to something in another, we are actually drawn to ourselves, our own attributes.

We do not feel drawn to or befriend someone who does not have our qualities.

But humans do change in time…

In time, our deeper qualities begin to manifest and our value judgments start to change. Our preference of friends differ… What we found valuable yesterday begins to lose meaning today. We begin to value things today that perhaps didn't mean much to us in the past…

Every bird flies with its own flock. Like attracts like and everyone eventually ends up with the people they attract and deserve!

A smart person is a realistic person. The *Haseeb* quality within us calls us to account in the guise of *Munkar* and *Nakir*.

That is when we realize, according to our knowledge, where and how we are spending our life…

I have encountered many people in my life… I have seen people who thought they were the spiritual leader of their time (*gaws*). Some of them kept seeing dreams of the **Rasul of Allah** (saw) or those close to him. Some of them ended up in mental illness hospitals, some of them ended up in denial, and some passed on with their illusions…

The important thing is, **how much of your knowledge are you able to put into practice and how much of your 'will' can you actualize with 'power' in accordance with 'knowledge'**… Not the number of nights you spend in illusion!

You came here alone and you will depart alone, only taking with you what you have gained in this worldly life... You will face the consequences of your actions alone, as you did in the past, as you are in the current moment.

Do not forsake your prayers from yourself, your friends and from me, someone whom you will probably never see.

26 August 2005
Raleigh – NC, USA

34

GOD'S MYSTERIOUS NIGHT OF POWER

Traditional religious approach, which is founded on **the concept of godhood**, imagines there is a night called the **Night of Power** (*Laylat al-Qadr*)'... A night on which, they claim, the almighty God blesses His select servants with a great bounty! Whoever worships and glorifies Him most gets the reward, the great reward called '*al-Qadr*'...

Apparently, the angels that bring down (!) this bounty descend to the region where Muslims live on the sacred night of power, for if they see daylight they will degenerate like spoilt vitamin C exposed to sunlight!

Apparently that night of power is more blessed than a thousand nights, or 83 years of deifying, glorifying and worshipping!

Every year on the 27th night of Ramadan, the angels flap their wings speedily to traverse a journey of thousands of years so they can descend to earth and go house to house to seek out the Muslims who happen to be in a time zone where it is night! Of course, the Muslims who happen to be in daylight at that instance of time miss out on everything. Too bad for them...

If the angels find a sincere worshipper they ask their Lord "Oh Lord! Shall we give this person *al-Qadr*?" If God says yes, they bless the person with *Qadir*, otherwise they move on to the next house. This house-to-house search to give out *al-Qadr* goes on till dawn... The believers, in the meantime, go from mosque to mosque hoping to get lucky!

How many people receive *al-Qadr* that night? Nobody knows...

What good does it do to those who receive *al-Qadr*? Nobody knows...

As soon as it's dawn and the sun begins to appear in the sky, the angels and the spirits immediately fly back to their homes near God!

***

According to Rasulullah-centered Islamic understanding, on the other hand, the construal of **the Night of Power** is as the following:

"Inna anzalnaHu fee laylatilQadr." (Quran 97:1)

The Quran, which is a reference to the **totality of secrets** and man's own **essence** (*anzalnaHU*), is revealed to man's consciousness when he experiences his **nothingness** (night).

Remember **man is the twin brother of the Quran**...

"Wa ma adraka ma laylatulQadr." (Quran 97:2)

Do you know what this reality, this secret (*al-Qadr*) is?

"LaylatulQadri khayrun min alfi shahr." (Quran 97:3)

Experiencing the darkness of your nothingness (night) during *al-Qadr*, is more auspicious than all that you can live in a thousand months (an 80 odd year life span).

"Tanazzal'ul malaikatu war Ruhu feeha Bi izni Rabbihim min kulli amr, salamun hiya hatta matla'il fajr." (Quran 97: 4-5)

The angels (**the angelic forces within – wings denote the 2-3-4 dimensions of these forces**) and the Spirit (**the meaning of 'HU' comprising the essence of your existence**) becomes revealed in one's consciousness with the permission (**capacity**) of his *Rabb* (**the composition of Allah's Names comprising his essence**); such that he experiences his inexistence **while experiencing the absolute existence of Allah**, in a state of certainty (*yakeen*) free from all judgments!

This state continues until his mind awakens and he begins to feel he is a separate existence again; until his human thoughts and feelings begin to 'dawn' on him.

"Seek the Night of *Qadr* every night of the year" means this opportunity should be sought every night, or every moment in which you feel your **inexistence** in respect of the One referenced by Allah!

"Seek it in the month of Ramadan" means one should seek to attain this state with the aid of **the true experience of fasting**, which cleanses man from his human ways and enables him to discover his reality!

"Seek it in the last ten days of Ramadan" means, seek it towards the end of your spiritual cleansing, **after a period of genuine fasting, as opposed to imitation**.

To summarize what the metaphors pertaining to the chapter **al-Qadr** mean:

One instance, in the lifetime of man, in which the knowledge pertaining to his essential reality is revealed from his essence to his consciousness through a leap or an expansion in consciousness, is far more auspicious then the entirety of his lifetime! For this reality is the reality pertaining to HU! Based on the principle: "Man is the secret of the Quran, the Quran is the secret of man" this reality is realized from the depths of man!

When?

When the person starts questioning who and what he is, when he believes in **Muhammad** (saw) **the Rasul of Allah**, and tries to understand his teachings and strives to cleanse himself from the concept of godhood by understanding Allah at least according to chapter *al-Ikhlas*...

When, in respect of the One whose name is Allah, he realizes the **inexistence** of his individual being, that is, when from the daylight of his existence, he falls into the darkness of his nothingness, and all forms lose their existence...

A moment in which he feels and experiences that the Names of Allah comprise and form his essence and when he realizes that

the Spirit, i.e. the meaning of the Names, and the angels, i.e. the forces of the Names, are ever manifesting through him!

This instance of realization is called the state of '*al-Qadr*'.

In this instance he no longer remains as an individual existence, nor does anything else in the conceptual world.

In this state he witnesses the verse:

"*...li manil Mulkul yawm Lillahi Wahidil Qahhar.*"

"**...To whom belongs all sovereignty this Day?** (this moment, now, in the sight of Allah time is only this present moment) **To Allah, the *Wahid*, the *Qahhar*** (The One whose absolute ruling applies beyond the concepts of time and space)**!**" (Quran 40:16)

He READS the "The Word of Testimony" (*Ash hadu...*) such that **the observer is none other than the Self!**

This state goes on until his mind-body self kicks in again and his human nature dawns on him.

He can now take his place among the people of reality as one who has experienced his own reality and begin to READ the secrets of the Quran as he awaits his death (change of dimension) **as a servant living his life according to his creation purpose.**

Why did I write this?

Because I believe **the Book** is not so much **a 'Book of God's Commandments'** as it is **a 'Book of Secrets'** which, if not **READ** properly, can leave one in severe deprivation...

This short chapter about ***al-Qadr*** is only one example out of many... There are countless other mysterious knowledge in the Book of Allah, especially one regarding **Ascension** (*miraj*), that needs to be deciphered and decoded in this light!

It is unfortunate that the majority of us are unaware of this profound knowledge, many of us still think of the Quran as God's book of commands and record of history.

I may be right, I may be wrong, but this is how I learned to read from the books written by the intimates of reality...

If I'm right, then those who do not evaluate this knowledge can think about their loss themselves…

If I'm wrong, then I am indeed in a lot of trouble by the almighty God sitting in the heavens sends His angels and spirit down to earth who once a year during some mysterious night of power!..

2 September 2005
Raleigh – NC, USA

35

DO NOT BE FOOLED!

Deception befalls us... Sometimes from an exterior enemy, sometimes from our own illusions!

External deceivers are easier to identify; beings who cannot tolerate humans for having higher values and attributes than themselves and want to pull them down from their higher human state as **"the most honored of creation"** to a carnal state of animalism! Beings who exploit their invisibility and take advantage of every weapon at their disposal!

Our internal deceiver, on the other hand, makes use of our lack of knowledge and discernment, our denial of our self and essence to punish us!

One pulls us away outwardly; the other buries us inwardly!

So, how can we save ourselves from this exhausting problematic situation?

The answer is simple: by **READing the '*Audhu...*'** protective prayer.

"But we repeat the *Audhu* a hundred times a day and nothing happens!? What kind of a state is this that even the constant repetition of the *Audhu* seems to be useless!?"

Of course it will be useless, my friend, 'repeating' the *audhu* like a tape recorder will have absolutely no benefit to you; the situation will 'repeat' itself forever!

First of all… We must be aware of the existence of other entities that are not visible to us. We must be cognizant of their ability to send certain impulses to our brain to affect our thought patterns!

Everything the **final Nabi and Rasul of Allah** (saw) taught has pertinence to recognizing the system and its mechanism in order to protect oneself (*taqwa*) and to know the reality of one's self!

The Rasul of Allah (saw) READ the system and wanted us to also be of the READers!

Therefore, in order to be among the protected ones we must first be among **the READers, not the 'repeaters'!**

In fact, we must stay as far away from repeating as possible!

The Rasul of Allah (saw) is to be read! The *sunnatullah* is to be read!

The *Audhu* is to be read! The Quran is to be read!

Since this is the case, let us READ the *Audhu* rather than repeating it. That is, instead of sporadically repeating the phrase **"Audhu billahi minash shaytanirrajeem"** thinking it's going to shield us against something, as is traditionally done, let us understand its meaning and read it consciously!

***Audhu*: I seek refuge…**

***B-illahi*:** in the protective forces of the Names of Allah comprising my Essence

***Minash shaytanir rajeem*:** from impulses generated by the **accursed and rejected (*rajim*)** Satan, which as a result of preconditionings, causes our sense of illusion to perceive the existent as non-existent and the non-existent as existent, thereby making man believe he is an independent being and body outside the Names of Allah, directing man to the idea of an external deity-God in the heavens.

To put it in other words:

I seek refuge in the forces of the Names and Attributes in my essence pertaining to the One whose name is Allah, from the one who has fallen away from their reality and wants to deceive and misguide me in vengeance of the fact that I have been created with a higher capacity!

Thus, to **READ the** *Audhu* with this comprehension is the second step...

The third step, after this comprehension forms, is to know how these invisible beings (with demonic attributes) deceive and misguide us...

Rather than listing their actions, I want to delineate their general philosophy:

The primary purpose of all invisible demonic entities, since **Iblis**, is to guide man away from his caliphate quality and reduce him from his 'most of honored of all creation' (*ashraf-i mahluq*) state, to a base, animalistic state of existence. In doing so, they wish to verify the arguments **"he is an animal created from soil"** and **"these humanoids/earthlings will spill blood and cause mischief on earth"**!

As such, **their fundamental principle is to divert man's attention to external things and prevent him from turning inward to his intrinsic qualities and potentials!**

They continually infuse man with thoughts of corporeality, making him think he is the body, or keep him busy him with his environment to trigger and nourish egoistic tendencies in him... They delude man into deifying and worshipping an external god and manipulate him to ask for things from this phantom god, to show him his prayers and requests are unanswered, thereby leading him to deny this imaginary god, which they label 'Allah'!

Their only aim is to prevent man from turning to his essential reality and deprive him of the qualities of the Names of Allah in his essence!

Thus, to drown a Sufi aspirant in the whirlpool of **the 'inspired self'** (*nafs-i mulhima*) **state of consciousness** is a perfect and simple solution for them!

'**Repetition**' implies evoking an external being, it entails tradition, conditioning, memorization and imitation.

'**READing**' on the other hand involves deciphering and decoding the system (*sunnatullah*) to understand its mechanism, and to output relevant THOUGHT and BEHAVIOUR.

This process of 'decoding/understanding and acting' is called '*iqra*' in the Quran, which means to READ!

Now…

If one realizes that a particular thought that appears in his consciousness is making him turn towards an external god or object and making him addicted or dependent on this object, then he is in danger of being misguided away from his own reality.

If he becomes conscious at this point, of the '*Audhu B-illah*' and '*Ista'eenu B-illah*' realities and reads them with the **intent of turning back to the One denoted by the name Allah in his essential reality**, and **seeks refuge in the forces comprising his essence**, he may be saved from the manipulations of the invisible beings and their attempts to suffocate him in the dangers of the external world.

If he fails to **READ**, he will inevitably succumb to being an object of their entertainment, as he awaits his death while they hurl and fling him in the treacherous ocean of corporeality!

What does it mean **to seek refuge in one's essential reality**?

This is revealed in the *Kul Audhu* prayers:

"***QUL***": recognize, realize, comprehend, experience and then say:

"***Audhu bi Rabbil falaq***": "I seek refuge in the *Rabb* (reality of the Names comprising my essence) of the *Falaq* (the light that prevails over the darkness and brings enlightenment to me)"

"***Min sharri ma khalaq***": From the evil of his creation

"***Wa min sharri ghasikeen idha wakab***": From the evil of the darkness that settles in my consciousness preventing me from perceiving and comprehending…

"Wa min sharrin naffathatee fil'ukad": From the evil of those who manipulate brainwaves to knots on a thread to make black magic...

"Wa min sharri hasideen idha hasad": From the evil eye of the enviers... (Quran 113:1-5)

"QUL": recognize, realize, comprehend, experience and then say:

"Audhu bi Rabbin Nas": "I seek refuge in the *Rabb* (reality of the Names comprising the essence) of the *Nas* (mankind)"

"Malikin Nas": The *Malik* (the One whose sovereignty and administration is absolute over) *Nas* (mankind)

"Ilahin Nas": The reality of *Uluhiyya* that resides within the essence of every human, with which he subsists his existence, and mistakenly thinks this state pertains to a god outside of himself!

"Min sharril waswasil hannas": From the evil of the whisperer that covertly pervades then retreats, and reduces man to corporeality

"Alladhee yuwas wisu fee sudurinnas": That which whispers illusory thoughts into man's consciousness about man's essential reality

"Minal jinnati wan Nas": From among the *jinni* and man... (Quran 114: 1-6)

In short, by reading these **protection** prayers we are seeking refuge in the **forces of the Names** in our essential reality and their ability to become manifest, from all things that are dark (things we don't perceive and understand) and from the evil of those who are involved in black magic (and who manipulate our brainwaves in this cause) and the negative energy of those who are envious...

Chapter *an-Nas* applies the principle **"the part reflects the whole"** and **"the hearts are in between the two fingers of Allah"** for the administration of one and the administration of a thousand are the same!

That is:

I seek refuge in the dimension of **'B'** *Rububiyyah* of my essence, which is also what forms the reality of all humans, thus, this act of seeking refuge on an individual level automatically takes effect at the level of humanity! I also seek refuge in the dimension of **Malikiyyah**, which rules over every individual consciousness at all instances! I also seek refuge in the *Ilah*, the One who created man with His Names and attributes... From those who deviously and slyly induce whisperings in my consciousness, which cause me to deny the Reality and make me restrict my existence to this flesh-bone body, causing me to live a carnal life driven to please the animalistic desires of my body!

Let us contemplate on these interpretations now... Let us try to understand them!

The absolute truth is this:

***"Illa B-iznihi"*!**

9 September 2005
Raleigh – NC, USA

36

SHATTERED TO PIECES

There is a popular phrase in Turkish that goes **"The man has an ego the size of a mountain!"** The word mountain obviously connotes enormity.

Ego, 'I'ness, selfhood all denote the same meaning. They all refer to the identity; **they all refer to 'I'**! The ego is a mountain of such enormity that it overshadows most other mountains!

Another such phrase is **"The sin of ego has overshadowed you the way a mountain would"** though this carries a slightly different meaning; it signifies the deification of one's own consciousness, the acceptance of one's 'self' as separate from the one that is referred to by the name Allah.

There is an important warning in the Book revealed to the Rasul of Allah (saw), in the last three verses of chapter *al-Hashr*, addressing especially this topic:

"Had We revealed this Qur'an (this truth) **upon a mountain** (the ego) **you would have seen it humbled and shattered to pieces in awe of Allah** (the realization of the nothingness of his ego or seeming 'self' in respect to the One denoted by the name Allah). **And these examples** (symbolic language) **We present to mankind so that they will contemplate."** (Quran 59:21)

Please don't say "You see? This just shows that the Quran is such an exalted book that, if it were to *descend* upon a mountain, the mountain would have ruptured, but man isn't aware of this"!

This verse isn't talking about a literal book and mountain! Only those who haven't yet cleansed themselves from the misconception of an external deity-god can perceive this verse so literally!

My understanding of this verse is as I wrote it above. And I am concerned about the **truth** mentioned in this verse, the powerful truth that, once it is comprehended, causes man's consciousness to be awe-struck, and shatters and wipes away even the biggest of egos!

What can this truth be? How can we attain it?

Allah, who is an absolute unknown in terms of His Absolute Essence (*dhat*), has created infinite forms of creation, and their activities, by manifesting the structural qualities denoted by His Names and Attributes, through the function of *Rububiyyah*!

"... **While it is Allah who created you and all your doings.**" (Quran 37:96)

'**You**' in this verse **is a reference to your Names**, i.e. your intrinsic qualities, **in the sight of the enlightened ones**. Anything that has a name, form or concept is essentially a compositional manifestation of His Names and Attributes, in the world of acts.

At every instance every unit of existence is *Hayy* (alive) and *Qayyum* (subsisting) with Him! **Every activity expressed through every individual is a unique composition of His Names.**

Since this is the case... When we refer to a quality pertaining to an individual we are actually referring to **the Names that are manifesting in the dimension of acts, or the realm of activity.**

Then let us realize that the same levels and dimensions are involved in the creation of every individual. Existence, with all its strata, is contained in all creation. Whether one uses religious allegory or scientific terminology, it is the same truth that is attenuated. A dimension in one exists in all! Their difference is in their manifestation... Thus, **Rasulullah**'s (saw) teaching **"the part** mirrors the whole" is not merely a key to a palace of secrets but it is the master key! It is the master key that opens not only the doors into the palace but all of the doors to the treasury rooms inside the palace too, given that it is in the hands of a qualified one.

The **Rasul of Allah** (saw) says**: "Allah has one less than a hundred, 99 Names. Whoever discerns their meanings will go to heaven…"**

1. **HU**
2. **AR-RAHMAN**
3. **AR-RAHIM**
4. **AL-MALIK**
5. **AL-KUDDUS**
6. **AS-SALAM**
7. **AL-MU'MIN**
8. **AL-MUHAYMIN**
9. **AL-AZIZ**
10. **AL-JABBAR**
11. **AL-MUTAKABBIR**
12. **AL-KHALIQ**
13. **AL-BARI**
14. **AL-MUSAWWIR**
15. **AL-GAFFAR**
16. **AL-QAHHAR**
17. **AL-WAHHAB**
18. **AR-RAZZAQ**
19. **AL-FATTAH**
20. **AL-ALEEM**
21. **AL-QABID**

22. **AL-BASIT**
23. **AL-KHAFID**
24. **AR-RAFI**
25. **AL-MU'IZZ**
26. **AL-MUDHILL**
27. **AS-SAMI**
28. **AL-BASIR**
29. **AL-HAKAM**
30. **AL-ADL**
31. **AL-LATIF**
32. **AL-HABIR**
33. **AL-HALIM**
34. **AL-AZIM**
35. **AL-GHAFUR**
36. **ASH-SHAKUR**
37. **AL-ALIY**
38. **AL-KABIR**
39. **AL-HAFIZ**
40. **AL-MUQEET**
41. **AL-HASIB**
42. **AL-JALIL**
43. **AL-KARIM**
44. **AR-RAQIB**
45. **AL-MUJIB**
46. **AL-WASI**
47. **AL-HAKIM**
48. **AL-WADUD**

49. **AL-MAJID**
50. **AL-BAITH**
51. **ASH-SHAHID**
52. **AL-HAQQ**
53. **AL-WAKIL**
54. **AL-QAWWI**
55. **AL-MATIN**
56. **AL-WALIYY**
57. **AL-HAMID**
58. **AL-MUHSI**
59. **AL-MUBDI**
60. **AL-MU'ID**
61. **AL-MUHYI**
62. **AL-MUMIT**
63. **AL-HAYY**
64. **AL-QAYYUM**
65. **AL-WAJID**
66. **AL-MAJID**
67. **AL-WAHID**
68. **AS-SAMAD**
69. **AL-QADIR**
70. **AL-MUQTADIR**
71. **AL-MUQADDIM**
72. **AL-MU'AKHKHIR**
73. **AL-AWWAL**
74. **AL-AKHIR**
75. **AZ-ZAHIR**

76. **AL-BATIN**
77. **AL-WALI**
78. **AL- MUTA'ALI**
79. **AL-BARR**
80. **AT-TAWWAB**
81. **AL-MUNTAQIM**
82. **AL-AFUW**
83. **AR-RA'UF**
84. **AL-MALIK'UL-MULK**
85. **DHUL-JALALI WAL-IKRAM**
86. **AL-MUQSIT**
87. **AL-JAMI**
88. **AL-GHANI**
89. **AL-MUGHNI**
90. **AL-MANI**
91. **AD-DARR**
92. **AN-NAFI**
93. **AN-NUR**
94. **AL-HADI**
95. **AL-BADI**
96. **AL-BAQI**
97. **AL-WARITH**
98. **AR-RASHID**
99. **AS-SABUR**

The key word in this hadith is **'discern'**!

Many misinterpret this as 'memorize' whereas what the Rasul of Allah (saw) is advising here is to understand the meanings denoted by these names and to **experience and observe their manifestations through one's self and the rest of creation!**

This naturally brings us to cleansing our self from the 'I'ness and adorning ourselves with the attributes of Allah!

Conspicuously, at this level of awareness, even an ego the size of **a mountain will be shattered to smithereens**!

Allah is *al-Baqi*! From pre-eternity, to post-eternity! There is no instance of inexistence pertaining to Him; He is the ever living one!

Notice the hadith above, where **Rasulullah** (saw) says: "**Whoever discerns these Names will go to heaven**" but he doesn't specify this event will take place **'after Doomsday'**! In other words, **going to heaven, is a metaphor for the bliss and happiness one can feel when one can understand the meanings of these names and identify their expressions through themself, as opposed to a hellish state of existence one endures through various pain and suffering**!

He who has believed, has believed in himself, and he who has denied, has denied himself!

To believe is to have faith in your reality (the unknown). **To deny is to cover up and refuse to realize one's essential reality**! For, what is pertinent to the **'reality'** is the meanings that are denoted by **His** names and attributes.

In regards to the last three verses of chapter *al-Hashr*, the **Rasul of Allah** (saw) **says: "Whoever recites the last three verses of chapter *al-Hashr* after reciting '*Audhu Billahis sami'al aleemi minash shaytanir rajeem*' in the morning, Allah will assign 70 thousand angels (forces) to him, who will send *salawat* to him until the day ends. If he dies that day, he will die as a martyr** (not staged martyrdom! One who gives up his corporeality at the expense of death for the sake of Allah...). **And it is the same for whoever reads these at night** (the effects will last till morning).''

So, what exactly is signified by these verses, which are so important to read, and which leave the mind in awe and, when comprehended, shatter the ego to pieces?

Why has the importance of their meaning been attenuated?

My understanding of these verses is:

HU is Allah, other than whom there is no deity (as HU is the inner essence of the reality of everything that is perceived).

The absolute Knower of the unknown and the witnessed!

HU is *ar-Rahman* (the potential of the source of the entire creation; the quantum potential encompassing all of the qualities of the Names),

Ar-Rahim (the One who manifests the infinite qualities denoted by the Names and experiences the world of acts with and through their observation),

HU is Allah, other than whom there is no deity (as HU is the inner essence of the reality of everything that is perceived),

HU is *al-Malik* (the Sovereign One who manifests His Names as he wishes and governs them in the world of acts as He pleases. The one who has providence over all things),

Al-Quddus (the One who is free and beyond being defined, conditioned and limited by His manifest qualities and concepts!),

As-Salam (the One who enables a state of emancipation from the conditions of nature and bodily life and endows the experience of 'certainty' (*yakeen*)),

Al-Mumin (the One who enables faith and guides individuals to observe their reality),

Al-Muhaymin (the One who observes and protects),

Al-Aziz (the One whose will to do as He likes, nothing can oppose),

Al-Jabbar (the One whose will is compelling),

Al-Mutakkkabir (the One to whom the word 'I' exclusively belongs. **Absolute 'I'ness** belongs only to Him),

Allah is *Subhan* (exalted and absolutely pure **from the god concepts they associate with Him!**),

HU is *al-Khaliq* (the ONE Absolute Creator! The One who brings individuals into existence from nothingness with His Names!),

Al-Bari (the One who fashions all of creation (from micro to macro) with unique functions and designs yet all in conformity with the whole),

Al-Musawwir (the fashioner of forms. The One who exhibits 'meanings' as 'forms' and devises the mechanism in the perceiver to perceive them),

To Him belongs the beautiful Names.

Whatever is in the heavens and earth extol (*tasbih*) **Allah** (by manifesting the qualities of the names comprising their essence, i.e. by actualizing their servitude),

HU is *al-Aziz* (the One whose will to do as He likes, nothing can oppose),

Al-Hakim (the One whose power of knowledge appears under the guise of 'causes', hence creating causality and leading to the perception of multiplicity). (Quran 59:22-24)

Indeed, there are profound depths of knowledge contained in these verses, but here I tried to outline only some of the meanings specifically relevant to the unity of Allah.

Salam to those brains with the capacity to contemplate beyond these meanings...!

Yes...

HU!

HU is the reality and essence, the **Rabb, Malik and Ilah** (the dimension of Uluhiyyah, or the Names and Attributes)!

HU is the actual SELF beneath the guise of the illusory self!

HU is the One, when failed to be recognized, leads to suffering and burning in a hellish state of existence!

HU comprises the essence of all beings, but if one fails to discern this they begin to worship deities postulated in their imagination and end up miserable!

HU is the One you can find in your own depths rather than in the skies!

HU is the essential reality of everything you perceive!

HU is the One, when recognized, will enable you to experience your 'nothingness' and 'inexistence' (zero point)!

HU is the One who, when man 'was a thing not worth mentioning', brought man into existence with His own structural, compositional qualities, who allows man to feel his 'nothingness' and enables him to live with this consciousness, and who will subdue man to eternal hell is he fails to live up to this reality!

HU is the One teaching you the secret to shatter your ego… If one consciously chooses to oversee this reality, then HU will make you blind to it altogether!

Come, my friend… Do not dissipate your mental energy on things that will have no benefit to you when death wakes you up and invites you to leave this world and all its belongings behind…

Do something for your eternal life!

Make some time to understand the Book of Secrets, the **Quran**, that has been disclosed to teach you about your own reality!

Think about what the **Rasul of Allah** (saw) brought to you, and why he has done so…

Remorse will be useless; you will never obtain this opportunity again!

If you fail to evaluate the knowledge contained in the **Magnificent Book**, the knowledge revealed about '**you**' in the absence of you, and Muhammad Mustapha, the **Rasul and the final Nabi of Allah** (saw), your end will be loss and disappointment alone!

For, when you change dimensions through death… You are going to see that…

The God you assumed existed… Was never true!

16 September 2005
Raleigh – NC, US

37

HOW WOULD YOU LIKE YOUR DREAM HOUSE TO BE?

Everyone has been promised a brand new house!

They are told: "You will leave your current homes and move into your new houses, if you believe in this promise. Start designing your houses as you like", the only condition is that no one can see their new house until they make the move.

Everyone, from a man living in the most remote little village to a skyscraper tenant in Manhattan, New York, is asked how they would like their dream house to be and all their requests are taken and applied exactly… Those full of doubt obviously do not have any requests… But those who take this offer seriously and put in the effort to design their new homes present their ideas and requests to the minute detail…. All of it is applied, everyone is given an equal chance; there is no injustice!

While a villager in a hamlet who lives with his cow in a tiny shed made with cow-dung excitedly dreams about owning a mud-brick house, just like those of the attractive neighboring village…

A New Yorker who lives in a remote controlled, computer-based, solar powered house and has the ability to connect and interact with all his friends around the world online, while his assistants run his errands and prepare his trip to Tokyo for dinner, is also eagerly imagining his dream home...

The villager is thinking:

"I want a house with mud-brick walls rather than cow dung... The ceiling should be made with solid wood not mud... The roof should be covered with nylon to prevent rain and snow from going in... It should have two rooms so my dear cow can have her own room right next door to mine... My house should have a nice round stove heater for winter... Aah yes.... And I would like fur filled quilt rather than this grass filled one! And, of course, a lamp instead of candles...."

And on goes the villager whose idea of luxury does not go beyond the mud-brick housed village up the road, whose biggest concern in life involves his cow's health, his sheep's milk and his hens' eggs, and whose only entertainment is the rumors that go on among the village folk...

The New Yorker is thinking:

"I'm tired of this still view of the city, I want to live in a mobile house now! I'm so over this computer system where the code doesn't cater for change in style... I want a smart house, one that will synchronize with my brainwaves and decode my thoughts to update itself according to what I'm thinking... I want an exclusive system in my house that enables me to see beyond my general visual field and protect me from negative energy vibrations that may be harmful... I want systems implemented in my house that will allow me to venture out to the infinite space and discover new beautiful places in the universe, systems that will empower me with health and vitality..."

The New Yorker doesn't care about the hustle and bustle of the town folk, he gives no importance to rumors, lies, accusations, power struggles, etc. His only concern is to make the best of this opportunity to design an ultimately efficient home in which he can reside and thrive...

As the story goes, the day finally comes and both men go to their custom-designed dream homes, leaving everything – their houses, friends and family, their environments and community – behind...

Both men find to their amazement, the home of their knowledge and vision, their ultimate dream home! Both are happy, and pursue their lives in bliss, totally unaware of each other...

As the old villager enjoys the pleasure of finally living in an advanced mud-brick house that for years filled his dreams, the urban ecstatically voyages to the unknown dimensions of outer space exploring his environment with his thought waves!

Some may deduce from this story that what's important is the house we design and go to, not the one we leave behind... Some may think of timber or concrete houses, and some may interpret it as the house of our consciousness, our bodies...

The truth is, it isn't as simple as believing you will be going to a new abode... In fact, to say "I believe in the hereafter" and to think this matters more than your current life is a serious misconception, as you are building and designing your home in the infinite hereafter every moment of your current life with the qualities you discover and express within yourself!

If you can say you are content with who you are today and do not feel the need to learn and discover new capabilities within yourself, that is fine too, it is your life my friend, the consequences of your choices will only bind you...

But if, on the other hand, you feel your cocoon is insufficient and you have the desire for a better life... If you are conscious of your ability to design your eternal abode with the divine qualities in your essence while still pursuing your earthly life... Then it is imperative for you to question and research everything you can and apply their requirements. You have to be open-minded and allow yourself to acquire new knowledge, and be adaptable!

For, **'Allah manifests Himself in yet another wondrous way every instance'**; He is forever creating anew. If you close yourself to change, you will be stuck in yesterday and indefinitely deprived of all the newness offered by today...

This is why **READing** the life guide **Quran** is our only aid... To **READ** the **Quran** in light of the letter **'B'** and attain the **'*Bi-zati-hi*'** to not just know, but experience it in person.

Oh friend! Tell me about the **mystery of the letter B**! Reveal to me its secrets...

Talk to me about the holographic view of seeing the whole in the part and the part in the whole!

Come, my friend... let us gaze at the letter **B** and its semblance...

First, a point is drawn and then it is extended to form a line, or the **'aleph'**...

Then this aleph is further extended and curved to form a semi circle and then another semi circle...

The point became a line; the line became two semi-circles on top of each other...

The top semi circle represents the **outer** (*zahir*) and the lower semi circle represents the **inner** (*batin*). Both semi circles obtain their existence from the line, the aleph, and the aleph is derived from the **point**.

So now we have two semi circles comprising a single line, which is ultimately a series of points, and due to its curvature and new shape, we give it a new name, and call it 'B'!

Now, let's examine the Arabic letter B, or Ba (ب), instead of the Latin one.

A broad and shallow semi oval and a single point beneath it!

This is what it looks like from a two dimensional view...

How about from a three dimensional view?

If we look at it from the bottom we can see the apex of a cone enlarging to its base on the top. A cone, projected from a single point! The cone contains the secrets and mysteries, all manifesting from the point!

Infinite cones projecting from one point, infinite cones within infinite cones!

Innumerous expressions of the Names as cones!

Fa tabarak Allahu ahsanul Halikeen!

Some perceive everything as two-dimensional and confine reality to their perception, claiming the point beneath the *Ba* is disconnected and separate... While others say **"I am a point, from the point... I am a cone comprised of innumerable points... I am a point that manifests many other points"**!

Whatever it means....

Discover the mystery of the 'B', my friend!

Ask yourself, why does **the Quran, which is a mirror to man**, begin with the letter **B**...

If **your twin brother, the Quran**, begins with the letter **B**, you must also begin all your activities and conduct your evaluations with the letter **B**... Most importantly, you must begin to know yourself through the letter **B**!

Expand your vision by knowing the Names constituting your essence!
Abandon your cocoon!

Transgress the two dimensional visual field (**eye**) and realize you are the multi-dimensional ***BASIR***!

Consciously say *B-ismi-Allah*.

Observe the *Rahman, Rahim, Halik, Muhyi* and others on the mirror of the Quran...

He made His names a mirror to you so that you may know yourself and design your eternal abode accordingly.

But alas! You have been squandering your life away with useless things! Losing your eternal life at the expense of what?

He said you are the caliphate, so that you may remember yourself, not so you think you are a master over others...

This world is just a dream, when you wake up in the other dimension you are going to realize this, but it is going to be too late to make any changes to your new abode.

Do not be deceived!

Leave others to themselves and get to **know yourself, discover your essence**, **expand your vision**, decode and express the forces and potentials with which you have been endowed through the mystery of the letter **B** and the mirror of the holographic view!

And remember,

Everyone has only one chance and one chance alone!

23 September 2005
Raleigh – NC, USA

38

THE COACH BUILDER

A man parked his car in front of the coach builder near the entrance of a small town to take a break... He saluted the builder, who was busily working on his next carriage... The coach builder took a quick glance at the man's white automobile, gave him a smile, then turning his nose up, he said: "Listen man, these satanic cars are dangerous things! You urbanites are quite keen but, take it from me, these cars will bring trouble to you! They may be faster than my carriages but, God forbid, they can tumble over! My carriages have spring suspension, they are very comfortable... I always make the seats soft and the wheels big, with one turn one can traverse quite a distance! You can go from here to the city at once; you don't need to worry about fuel either! You can open the awning if it rains or if its too sunny, and you have the option of riding without the awning if you want to enjoy the scenery... The bridles are made from fine leather; they are durable yet gentle on your hands, plus my carriages are designed for two carthorses, so you can travel long distance as well! We put in a lot of science and innovation into our carriages, the perimeter of the wheels, the balance, the height, all of this requires a lot of calculation... We believe in the carriage trade and keep up to date with new improvements..."

As they were talking, the townfolk had gathered around them... Listening to the old carriage maker they nodded their heads in agreement... With this support, the coach builder went on even further about the quality of his carriages and how easy they are to ride and how the townfolk use his carriages to leisurely visit the neighboring villages, and how they can even carry their personal belongings in the basket on the back of the carriage and on and on.... As he bragged about his carriages, the townfolk listened admiringly and even felt proud to have such an establishment in their town... But, of course, they didn't want to be rude to their visitor who came in a chunk of white metal either, so they offered him a drink... The visitor observed the crowd in silence and listened patiently, then politely said: "Good on you, my friend, you are doing a great job... May Allah increase your strength and success... How happy for you, both you and your fellow men are pleased, may you live in peace and in good health" then parted from the crowd and went into his white car...

In 16 seconds he lowered the hard-top roof of his convertible, and with one push of a button he started his car. He checked his rear from his navigation screen to make sure no children were in his way, then waved to the crowd as he took off in his 7 gear 493 horsepower, 516 ft/lbs of torque mechanical marvel, and disappeared in seconds!

The villagers were awe-struck as they watched him leave; it was as though they had seen a ghost!

The carriage maker was still going on about the beauty and versatility of horse carriages as though he had not even seen the man and his white car...

And the villagers went back to listening in admiration and envy as though they hadn't just seen the visitor and his spectacular car...

***

After sharing this story with you, I would like to draw your attention to the following:

An increasing number of Muslims, leaving Islam aside, are looking into Buddhism and other such beliefs, claiming Buddhism is the reality of Sufism and one can attain nirvana by saying "Aum"...

Aah, my darlings... My dear friends who think Islam is what the so-called Muslims reflect, and go out of their way to find solace in

Buddhism or in Christianity by worshipping Jesus, thinking God's son is going to come down in a spaceship to take them to his Father!

How can we blame them? They deserve some empathy… Here is this religion called Islam, which supposedly claims there is a God in space that goes by the name Allah, with a two-pan scale to weigh the sins and virtues of people and whoever doesn't dress and grow a beard like Abu Jahil and Abu Lahab are thrown into the hellfire! A religious *shariah* founded on a hundred thousand '*fatwas*' released every year over 1,400 years!

Surely the intellectual ones don't want to have anything to do with this!

How can the light of Islam be seen through this horrid dust cloud!

Not everyone has the means and circumstances with which I have been blessed, to dedicate 40 years of their life to search for the reality of Islam!

The truth is the sun of the Quran and Islam shines upon humanity, encompassing and addressing everyone, until the end of time, no matter what their background may be!

But no matter how bright the sun shines, when the clouds fill the sky, one is left in the shadows! Clouds can even block the view of one's path! The only solution is to walk away from the dark cloudy place and seek out clear skies…

When the sun, signified by the Rasul of Allah (saw), is overshadowed by primitive, shallow, formalist and martial mentalities, quite naturally, many people want to escape, and hence, adhere to Buddhism or Christianity, in search of tolerance and love!

If only we can see the **Rasulullah** sun, the monument of love who said: **"Facilitate, don't make things hard for yourself, promote love, not hatred"**… If only we can see the magnificent man who dedicated his life to saving the eternal lives of people…

If only we can recognize this amazing person who said: **"there is no god in the skies, do not waste your time in expectation from external things you deify and worship, seek the One denoted by the name Allah, who is ever present within every iota of** existence, the One who resides within your every cell, your essence, heart and consciousness"...

Whether male or female, each and every one of us is a caliphate on this earth... If only we can understand the Rasul of Allah (saw), who most ideally manifested the Names of Allah and tried to show us their beauty!

If only we can truly evaluate the Nabi of Allah who said: **"If two Muslims draw swords against each other, both the killer and the killed are in hell"** and **"If someone claims another to be an unbeliever, and his claim is false, he will become an unbeliever himself"**...

And if only we can discern the most magnificent aspect of it all... Which is the fact that the path from our self to the reality of our self, through ascending (*miraj*) to Allah is, again, via our very own essence...

It is an external journey called the 'laws of nature' that begins from our brain, enabling us to know our bodies and the extension of our bodies, our spirits and the laws that govern them, to finally allowing us to recognize the universal realities!

If only we can be cleansed from the archaic illusion that 'everything is confined to what is visible; what is not visible does not exist'!

If only we can save ourselves from the narrow minded view that 'the earth is flat, and god is in the heavens with his 3-5 winged angels and all he cares about is casting humans and *jinn* into hellfire, the earth is in the center of the universe and everything is created to serve man' and recognize the magnificent creation system called the *sunnatullah* disclosed by the **Rasul of Allah** (saw)...

If we could just grasp the reality that the **One denoted by the name Allah is present with His names in every iota and that His administration and dominance is expressed from the essence of every being**...

If only we knew that the practices known as prayer are not for a deity-god but for the individual to know themself and thereby reach Allah, and their external aspect aids in the speedy formation of the conditions to form one's eternal life, which again, requires the activation and expression of the intrinsic divine qualities inherent within...!

The magnificent brain of the **Rasul of Allah** (saw) manifested the qualities of *Risalah* and *Nubuwwah* in the most comprehensive way to show us the **universal mechanism and its function; how and what things are formed, what events will be lived and how can one take necessary precautions...**

If only we could read, through insight, the manual of the universal system; the magnificent Book of Knowledge and its timeless truths!

Aah, my friends... Which of these shall I explain?

If I were to share my insights in detail each of these can be a book on their own...

During my youth I used to pull my TK 145 tapes apart and put them back together following its instruction manual... Then when the cathode ray tube TV came out, I used to change the electron gun and readjust the tube... I had a 1303 Volkswagen beetle; I would dismantle its carburetor to clean it and then configure its air intake and valve adjustments... Fixing a typewriter was the easiest... Then the personal computers came out and I owned one with a 2 MB hard disk, the most advanced computer of its time... And now, I use an ASUS P5AD2-e board, 4 GB RAM SATA computer...

I have lived my entire life relying only on myself. I didn't spare any area of knowledge, from atom physics to chemistry, from medicine to psychiatry... I researched all of it, just for the sake of better understanding **religion** ...

I realized to appreciate and comprehend religion and the **Quran** one needs all of this knowledge, for each of these fields constitute a gear in a magnanimous mechanism that works as an integrated system, created by Allah!

I don't know if there is a hadith or Sufi book that I have not yet read...

I even observed 90-120 day diets and fasted for 3-5 days consecutively, without making *iftar* in between, because **Ahmad**

Rufai and **Bursawi** advised one must practice this knowledge if one wants to discern it…

In short, there are very few things that I haven't tried or experienced on my life path, following the footsteps of the **Rasul of Allah** (saw)…

I was threatened and agitated by many, but I placed my belief and trust in Allah alone.

For, he who is not open to the new has no chance of attaining the new!

New things become apparent coupled with new applications!

Old methods cannot yield new products! Every new product is produced by a new method; the new can never be obtained via the old, according to my understanding.

I didn't let anyone's conception limit me, I always searched for a new way, I took their views into account but I only walked on my own path; the path bestowed to me by Allah, with **His knowledge, will and power**…

This is how I came to be who I am today. Now I am waiting the day when I can leave this world with the peace of having done my best to understand the **Rasul of Allah** (saw), the system he disclosed and the **Quran** he imparted, according to my capacity…

I pray that you also reach peace and tranquility through the *dhikr* **of Allah**…

For, the 'heaven' of knowing Allah cannot be experienced anywhere else!

Whatever you achieve and acquire pertaining to this world will eventually come to an end, which for a thinker is unsatisfactory and depressing.

But the journey in Allah with Allah is eternal and ever exciting!

Oh phoenix birds who are trying to escape your cocoons to fly out to eternity!

Realize that you are not little sparrows, and be certain that you never be satisfied with small prey…

27 October 2005
Raleigh – NC, USA

39

THE FUNCTION OF THE REVIVER

While the titular Muslims, who haven't succeeded in comprehending the reality of the phenomenon of **religion**, and think of it as the commands of a distant God, squander their lives with shallow and formalist mentalities; they are utterly unaware of all the activities of **the Reviver of their time!**

Here is a summary of my understanding of the Reviver's purpose and function:

The **Reviver**, who (according to Imam Rabbani, Said Nursi and Kushadali) has commenced his duty between the Hijri years 1400-1410 (Gregorian 1970-1989), has already instigated an unmatched renewal in every area in the world...

Preceding Revivers, similar to Nabis and Rasuls that came to specific tribes or nations, served to correct the misconceptions pertaining to faith related issues of classical religious understanding...

The Reviver of our time, on the other hand, is here to serve as the representative of the Rasul of Allah (saw) and, hence, to address the whole of humanity, renewing and regenerating the lives and values of everyone and revitalizing the concept of religion, universally.

Despite the obliviousness of the great majority, the regenerative waves he has been emanating to the world since the 80s are being perceived by the brains that are receptive to that frequency and processed according to their natural disposition (*fitrah*) to produce various outcomes...

Some such receivers around the world, from Turkey to the United States, from South Africa to the Muslims in the East, have even thought they are the '*Mahdi*' or 'custodian or 'Reviver' and have consciously or inadvertently implied this to their surroundings. However, such people have nothing to do with the kind of revitalization I am referring to.

The true Reviver is not even known by the saints of our time! For he is concealed under the veil of Allah; only a portion of his activities can be recognized.

What matters for me is to recognize his activity and function and see what he has to offer, rather than knowing who he is.

As far as I'm aware, he is already serving humanity to reveal the light of Muhammad (saw), and anyone who receives the waves he emits is actively **dispelling the clouds in between and directing people to the Rasul of Allah** (saw) **and the Quran.**

The **Muhammadan** way is to share what you have **unrequitedly**, not to make profit! Hence, the receivers of his waves, whatever their religious or cultural background may be, share their knowledge to guide people to this reality without expecting any return! Here is an example from the world of technology:

LINUX!

Many of my readers are probably not even aware of this system.

Linux is an operating system, developed as an alternative to Microsoft's Windows. Windows is a system symbolic of that which is left from our ancestors, full of bugs that need constant fixing and updating. Linux on the other hand, has only been around since the early 90s and was developed with the knowledge and research of its developers and presented to the community for free.

Windows works only on computers that run on Intel or AMD platforms, just like the limited brains that only operate with the conditionings and indoctrinations of the 'Quran courses' and 'Religious Institutions'!

Linux is platform free! It operates on all platforms from Apple, Amiga and Sun Sparc, to the world's fastest computer IBM BlueGene/L and others… **Just like the brains that are able to evaluate the knowledge imparted by the Rasul of Allah** (saw) **and observe the One denoted by the name Allah on the engendered existence without any restrictions!**

The Windows operating system cannot be changed – one must use it as it is. You can't even share it with others, **you either comply with the Windows operating system absolutely, or you don't use it at all. You are either a part of the Windows community or you are an outcast!**

Linux, however, can be configured and personalized by its user to suit the user's needs and it can be used to serve many purposes. The kernel can be edited and updated by anyone. There are no limits on the number of users and its code is open to be examined, edited and personalized by everyone, so long as the user has enough coding knowledge. Even if the user doesn't possess sufficient knowledge, he can ask someone else to do it for him, and then share this new code with the community. There are no copyright restrictions on the system; it is openly available to the public in every version.

One must pay money to obtain Windows (just like the institutionalized religious schools and courses). **Linux, however, is a gift to humanity**. **It is free knowledge, shared with the community unrequitedly; it is not owned or copyright restricted. You do not need to make any payments to anyone to obtain and use this system.**

The source code is hidden in Windows, the user is unaware of which codes can lead him where while using this system. With Linux, the source code is open; the user is not dependent on any medium to achieve their goals.

Windows offers no options to its users; one does not have the right to question or ponder the system. You must accept it unconditionally, and once you do you no longer need to use your brain to develop it, it is a fixed code.

With Linux, on the other hand, you have the right to question the code, search the code and, if need be, develop and change the code. And you do not have to give account to anyone, the only condition is to not restrict copyright on your version and share it freely with the community.

To survive on the Windows platform you must be a servant to the system.

In the Linux system, however, everyone is free, everyone draws their own path and faces their own consequences!

Windows is the easy way out, with a few clicks one can use the system and, without having to put further thought into it, one can continue using the system imitating the same few clicks here and there to achieve 'satisfactory' results!

The Linux environment, however, encourages innovation and newness, it encourages contribution and sharing.

Windows resembles the traditional Muslim understanding based on conditioning and imitation.

Linux signifies the original system of the Rasul and final Nabi of Allah (saw) who encouraged people to question and research. It represents a one-on-one association with the Rasul of Allah (saw)! It is a system for individuals who seek to discover everything within themselves and who do not put mediators between themselves and Allah.

So, through an example of how it manifests in the computer world, I tried to illustrate my understanding of the innovation the Reviver of our time brings to this world.

Think about how this system is concealed yet so effective. Many people haven't even heard of it, yet have been benefiting from it without even being aware... Many confine the computer world to the Windows operating system alone and observe 'innovation' only as much as Windows allows them to.

Yet these words are reaching you now via a Linux operating system...

This is how the **Reviver** is concealed!

Who knows if I'll live long enough to see the new waves, new understandings and innovations the **Reviver** brings. Or perhaps I already have and I don't know!

In short, we need to cleanse and refresh our understanding of the **Reviver** and stop anticipating a *Mahdi* with a sword or a preacher of religion, and realize he is **a universal servant of Allah** sent to our world, just like the **Rasul of Allah** (saw), and he is here to address all of the nations in the world, to invite everyone to a better understanding, a better state of existence…

7 November 2005
Raleigh – NC, USA

40

READ ANEW

After parting from the small town where I live in the US and giving conferences throughout London, Paris, Berlin, Hamburg, Gelsenkirchen, Dusseldorf and Amsterdam, I have been blessed with the opportunity to take some time off in Turkey, and spend Ramadan here with my friends. I am thankful to the One who has bestowed on me this opportunity…

My intention for hosting these conferences, the last of which I will be conducting tomorrow, is not to teach you something; for I am sure there are among you people who are more knowledgeable then myself, but to assist you to view things from a different perspective, and help you realize you are not limited to your present perception.

My favorite verses in the Quran are those that are seemingly contradictory. For it is these verses that contain the biggest secrets! As soon as I read a verse that seems contrary to my conditioned mind I know out of experience it contains many hidden secrets, so I dive right into it!

If we want to gain a serious, consistent and logically complete understanding of the Quran and recognize it for the treasure chest of secrets it is, then we must evaluate the knowledge it contains with consistency and logic.

If the Quran is approached with preconceived notions or with the intention to confirm hearsay ideas, nothing can be gained from it. One must approach the Quran as though it is their first time reading it and try to understand its message without any predetermined views.

For example, when reading the chapter *al-Ikhlas* if one perceives it as dual relationship between a God and His servant, rather than the Absolute Oneness and Unity delineated by these verses, this shows an inadequacy of a holistic approach and logical completeness.

There is a general notion among non-Arabic speakers that the Quran should not be read in its Latin transliteration. Allow me to clarify this: It is almost impossible for someone over their 30s or 40s to learn to read in Arabic like an Arab, nor is it necessary. It is important to note that words are repeated first in the brain then via the tongue. That is, the shape of the letters is perceived by the brain as waves of electric signals, which are then decoded in the brain and linked to the letters in its database. They are given a form with the expression of the name *al-Musawwir* and converted into an image and then sent to the tongue via the larynx. The tongue is the final stage in this process. The crucial point is not the forming and shaping of the incoming message, but the deciphering and decoding of its meaning. The process up to this point is the same for all humans around the world, the output stage however, that is, the point from the larynx to the tongue, differs with region.

For the thinking brain, it is the meaning the brain takes in that matters most, while for the materialistic ones who can't comprehend the depth of the matter, it is only what the tongue projects or what their eyes see that is taken to account when evaluating religion.

Henceforth, I recommend you read the Quran in whichever language is most easy for you and concentrate on the **meaning of its words** rather than their alphabetic shape. This is the conclusion I have come to after spending over 40 years of exploration and study.

Let us now inquire into the first verses of the chapter *al-Baqarah*, in respect of the **oneness** (non-duality) elucidated in the chapter *al-Ikhlas*, and in the light of the letter 'B' as expounded by **Hadhrat Ali** (ra)…

"Alif, Laam, Meem. Dhalikal Kitabu larayba feehi hudan lil muttakeen." (Quran 2:1-2)

As I had noted before, what the word Book in Arabic (*Kitab*) signifies is Knowledge rather than a literal book. Therefore:

"This is the Knowledge (Book) **of Reality and *sunnatullah*** (the mechanics of the system of Allah)**, about which there is absolutely no doubt, it is the source of comprehension for those who seek protection...."**

"Alladheena yu'minuna Bilghayb wa yukeemunas salatah wa mimma razaknahum yunfiqoon."

"Who believe in the reality (that their being is comprised of the compositions of the Names of Allah) **unknown to them** (beyond their perception)**, and who establish prayer** (who experience the meaning of *salat* alongside performing its physical actions) **and who spend from both the physical and spiritual sustenance of life that We have provided for them unrequitedly for the sake of Allah."** (Quran 2:3)."

"Walladheena yuminuna Bi ma unzila ilayKa we ma unzila min kablK(A) wa Bil akhirati hum yukinoon."

"And who believe in what has been revealed to you from your essence (from the depths of your essence to your consciousness) **and what was revealed before you, and who, of their eternal life after, are certain** (in complete submission as a result of an absolute comprehension)**."** (Quran 2:4)

"Ulaika ala hudan min Rabbihim wa ulaikal humul muflihoon."

"They are in a state of HUDA (comprehension of the reality) **from their *Rabb*** (the name composition comprising their essence) **and it is they who have attained emancipation."** (Quran 2:5)

Now let us have a look at the meaning of the *Ayat al-Qursi*, the popular verse generally read for protection... According to my understanding, the *Ayat al-Qursi* reveals the various stations and levels of the names and attributes of Allah manifested on man. It begins from the station of absolute essence of Oneness (*Ahadiyyah*) the essential reality of man, and delineates all of the various stations up until the physical body...

Allah – there is no deity God, only HU!

Al-Hayy (The infinite source of names! The One who gives life to the Names and manifests them. The source of universal energy, the essence of energy).

Al-Qayyum (The One who renders Himself existent with His own attributes, without the need of anything. Everything in existence subsists with *al-Qayyum*).

Neither drowsiness overtakes Him (disconnection from the worlds even for a single instance) **nor sleep** (leaving creation to its own accord).

To Him belongs whatever is in the heavens and whatever is on the earth (everything transpiring within the dimensions of knowledge and acts).

Who can intercede with Him except by the permission (*Bi-iznihi*) **of the force of the Names comprising his essence** (the force that manifests from them)?

He knows the dimension in which they live and the dimension they are unable to perceive...

Nothing of His knowledge can be conceived if He does not will (allow via the suitability of the Names in one's essence).

His *Qursi* (sovereignty and administration [*Rububiyyah*]) **encompasses the heavens and the earth,**

And their preservation tires Him not.

And He is *al-Aliy* (The Highest. The sublime One who observes existence from the point of reality (essence) **and** *al-Aziz* (The One who, with His unchallengeable might, disposes as He wishes). (Quran 2:255)

This is my understanding of the *Ayat al-Qursi* in respect of its manifestation on the individual... Of course, there is also its meaning in respect of the universal dimension, as every verse has both an internal and an external meaning according to the Rasul of

Allah (saw). By all means you can research other translations and interpretations by those with whom you share the same vision.

October 2005
Expo Channel Conferences

41

FAREWELL

My dear friends,

Those who haven't encountered others like me naturally ask me:

"What is your purpose, what are your expectations, what do you want to achieve?"

I don't know how else to clarify this. Here is my answer:

None of my work is copyright restricted and I ask for no price for it. I freely share all of the knowledge on my site (www.ahmedhulusi.org) with the sole purpose of aiding a better understanding of the One denoted by the name Allah, as disclosed and expounded by Muhammad (saw), and a correct evaluation of religion based on this vision. All of my work can be freely read, listened to, watched, downloaded, reproduced (with the condition of citing the author and source) and distributed via individual and social mediums of communication over the internet or in other ways. The material cannot be reproduced for the purpose of selling without written consent. There is no recompense for the knowledge of Allah. My principle is to share freely, without any return, material or non-material.

I have no requests from anyone for my work and there will be no material inheritance left after me when I die either. For I have no foundation or organization; I do not collect any donations; I have no trusts or institutions!

I am not a member of any organization, foundation, association or institution of any sort. I carry no ties to any worldly organization, and have nothing to do with any political regime whatsoever.

I do not invite anyone to a particular order or myself! In fact I always say: "Please do not call me! If you benefit from my works then turn to Muhammad Mustapha, the Rasul of Allah (saw) with sincerity and purity, try to know him!"

I say do not try to contact me, you cannot reach me! This is why I haven't used my last name on any of my books since the 60s, I only use my first and middle names. I have no email address. I do not have a representative to talk on my behalf or make interpretations. Whoever attempts to do so will only be sharing their own ideas, not mine. All of my ideas are either written or as they have been recorded on audio and video mediums.

The black background of the front cover of my books represents darkness and ignorance, while the white color of the letters represents light and knowledge.

The image is a Kufi calligraphy of the Word of Unity: **"*La ilaha illallah*; Muhammad Rasulullah" which means, "There is no concept such as 'god', there is only that which is denoted by the name Allah, and Muhammad (saw) is the Rasul of this understanding."**

The placement of the calligraphy, being on top and above everything else on the page, is a symbolic representation of the predominant importance this understanding holds in my life.

The green light, reflecting from the window of the Word of Unity, opens up from the darkness into luminosity to illustrate the light of Allah's Rasul (saw). This light is embodied in the book's title through my pen and concretized as the color white, to depict the enlightenment I aim to attain in this field. As the knowledge of Allah's Rasul disseminates, those who are able to evaluate this knowledge attain enlightenment, which is represented by the white background of the back cover.

Farewell

I am aware that my language can be inadequate in expressing certain truths. But I am not worried as I am doing my best to share a different perspective. The sheer pleasure of this service is sufficient for me. By all means, you are free to take this much further...

As I always say, the religion of Islam has come to teach man about the universal system and order of Allah. If man can comprehend this system and its mechanics, he can discern his place and his future conscientiously. This discernment will enable him to conquer his eternal afterlife. For, man can only shape his afterlife now, in this earthly life, via specific spiritual practices and exercises based on the system of Allah.

As such, the biggest gift one can give to humanity is knowledge that will aid in successfully acquiring a blissful afterlife.

He who knows himself and Allah will be at peace with the whole of humanity, regardless of race, color, religion, language differences... he will embrace all of them with love and compassion, he will not deceive them.

He who knows Allah will not have any expectations from people; Allah will be sufficient for him! He will recommend the good and await the end of his days with patience and tolerance. He will know that all things serve their creation program and in the absolute sense, everything is in servitude to Allah. He will know that whether one is a baron, a count, a governor or a saint, it does not matter; every soul will taste death and make the transition from this material world into a new dimension alone. Every person will inescapably see the return of his earthly deeds. As such, it is imperative to know the system of the afterlife if one wants to adequately prepare for it!

Good days and bad days on earth will eventually come to pass, but an **eternal life** after the transformative event known as death...?

This is why, disregarding all worldly values and conditionings, I chose to share the knowledge of reality with people. The insightful ones will know who I am and what I do. As for the people of externality, they need not know anyway! I have no expectations from anyone; I am simply sharing my knowledge, not imposing it! The Rasul of Allah (saw) never imposed or enforced his knowledge; who am I to? Just as the lifestyles and preferences of others are not my business, my lifestyle and preferences are also nobody's business. Because I am not the example, Muhammad Mustapha, the Rasul of Allah (saw), is the example!

He is a sun, an infinite source of light, enlightening the lives of people!

I, on the other hand, am like a meteor, emerging temporarily from the depths to shed some light into the sky of your consciousness throughout the month of Ramadan, before becoming extinguished and disappearing! Like a shooting star granting a wish to its observer... So transitory... Stand to prayer when you see this star in your sky! Take ablution and perform two *rakahs* of *salat* in solitude, then make a prayer in prostration...

Say: "O Allah! The *Rabb* of the *Arsh*, the Spirit, and all of the angels! I pray to you with the consciousness that I am nothing in your presence; I am inexistent! O Allah, please enable me to comprehend your reality, please forgive me for all of the mistakes I have made inadvertently and out of weak will!

O Allah, the *Rabb* of Muhammad (saw)! Facilitate for me, the path of those you have favored and blessed, and protect me from becoming misguided! Honor me by putting me among the chosen ones. Befriend me with those you love most, and ease their practices for me also, make me of the beloved ones! Facilitate the experiencing of the realities you have bestowed to your beloved ones, show me my mistakes and help me to correct them.

O Allah, other than whom nothing exists! O Allah, who creates everything with perfection, and whose comprehension is impossible! *Ya Hu Ya men Hu*?

For the sake of your Absolute essence, save my perception from blindness, enable me to discern the absolute reality, and allow me to fathom it! Bless me with such certainty that no form of doubt or duality (*shirq*) can ever find way into my heart again!

O Allah! I seek refuge in you from whatever may be impeding my experience of approaching the absolute reality (*Haqq al-yakeen*). I seek refuge in you from you! I seek refuge from being in your presence with a sense of self (identity). You are the protector and your power overrides all things. You are the *Rabb* of the worlds, the *Azim*!

Help me to deservedly and duly know your Rasul, who taught these truths to us. Bless him with the utmost of blessings, however he deserves it, for we are impotent from duly praising him"...

And keep praying as it comes from your heart while prostrating... Know that your prayers will reach the One in your essence, and your *Rabb* **will answer you... From you, have no doubt!**

Other than sharing my knowledge with you, I repeat, **I am no man of religion, theologian, sheikh, scholar or a leader! Nor do I have any other labels!** I am merely a simple man living a simple life, though a great devotee of the Rasul of Allah (saw)! I have many faults, mistakes, and shortcomings... I suffer from the pain of not duly knowing the **Rasul of Allah** (saw), and his disclosure of **Allah** and the *sunnatullah*!

I try my best to explain the magnificent truth to you as plainly and clearly as I possibly can but it seems the messages that are taken are very different. Here are two examples of which I have become aware:

A man is advised by his friend to watch one of my videos. He begins watching, a short while later he turns it off, calls his friend and swears at me, saying: "He literally says there is no God! Why on earth would you advise this kind of thing to me!?"

The second example is about my friend's 6-year-old daughter, Ozdenur. Apparently when her parents were watching one of my videos, she was sitting on her father's lap with her eyes closed. Her parents thought she was sleeping. Two days later her mother witnessed a conversation Ozdenur was having with one of her peers. Her friend was very upset with someone and was saying: "I'm going to complain about her to Allah!" pointing her finger to the sky. Upon hearing this, Ozdenur said: "Allah is not in the sky, why are you pointing up?" Her mother was astounded; she had thought Ozdenur was asleep during the video. Then her friend asked: "Then where is Allah?" and Ozdenur replied: "Allah is inside us all"...

So they ask me: "Why haven't we heard any of this before?"

Because you couldn't! Because my works are heavily censored in Turkey. In certain places, even mentioning the name Ahmed Hulusi is prohibited. The Turkish Ministry of Religious Affairs has banned my books from being sold; the books I have been printing and freely distributing for over 40 years! My audios and videos are prohibited from being published or broadcasted! If any of my works were to be accidentally broadcasted in any way, they will be removed immediately by the powers that be. Hence, Ahmed Hulusi need not live in Turkey!

On the other hand, there are those who claim I bring a new age and moderate version of Islam from America...

It is funny how people are so prejudiced and so quick to judge... It is not even worth responding to such accusations...

Ahmed Hulusi's stance is quite conspicuous. Go and read my book *Revelations*, an account of my insights at the age of 21, written in 1966. Go and read *The Mystery of Man* written in 1985. Or read **Muhammad's Allah**, originally written in 1989. You will see that Ahmed Hulusi has kept the same stance for 42 years with no digression, and he has shared all of it without asking for anything in return. So here you have it, you have listened to me throughout this month of Ramadan, everything I have shared is at your disposal. Why they would censor this material, I leave that to your discretion.

My friends...

Take this knowledge, use it and then leave me! You have no business with me, your business is with the most magnificent form of consciousness that has ever transpired on earth, Muhammad Mustapha (saw)!

Apply your knowledge to the best of your understanding and experience its result! Know that no excuse is going to be valid in the afterlife! Such and such person who led you astray is not going to hold any validity on the other side! Each soul is going to live the results of their own deeds!

Do not let the colorful world of the *Dajjal* (Antichrist) deceive you! In his world, mortals are disguised as immortals and the wrongs as rights! That which is worthless in the infinite realms is made to appear as valuable in his finite world! To harbor his fraud and prevent the reality from becoming apparent, new prohibitions are brought by the powers that be, preventing people from thinking and questioning! People are like herds of sheep in their view, and they are the shepherds!

Gain your liberty my friends! Start thinking, questioning, and re-evaluating your knowledge to better understand the Quran and the magnificent Rasul of Allah (saw).

I'm extending a hand of help...

Free yourself from the hundred million *fatwas* released since **Hadhrat Ali** (ra). Listen only to the **Rasul of Allah** (saw) and define the direction of your life based on his teachings alone. There are millions of people around the globe from different regions who unanimously believe there is no god, there is only Allah. Can all these people, who accept the Rasul of Allah (saw) and the Quran, be called irreligious or unbelievers just because they are unaware of the tens of thousands of *fatwas*, or have not joined a Sufi order and aren't accustomed to a *mazhap*? Please use your intellect and logic and question religion realistically!

Let us know with certainty that anyone who has accepted the Rasul of Allah (saw) and the teachings in the Quran is a believer, even if all the Muslims in the world were to call him an unbeliever!

Let the only person to whom you submit be the most magnificent person to have ever walked this earth, the **Rasul and final Nabi of Allah, Muhammad Mustapha** (saw)!

A Christian cannot turn to God without the church and the Vatican! A Jew cannot turn to God without a rabbi! A Muslim, on the other hand, needs no religious institution, mufti, sheikh, leader nor the government! Turn your face to the Rasul of Allah wherever and whenever... Turn to Allah in your essence; do not put any mediators in between!

Our biggest difference from the Christians and Jews is about Muhammad (saw). They do not believe he is the Rasul of Allah and, as such, far from Allah as disclosed by him, they believe in an external deity-god up in the heavens; a god that is soon to descend to the earth! Whereas Muhammad's difference lies here! He removed all vehicles and mediators between man and

Allah by disclosing the reality of Allah. The Bible is equivalent to a book of hadiths not to the Quran, for it comprises a record of the accounts of Jesus' apostles; they are not revelations like the verses in the Quran! How much of the 'good news' (bible) actually revealed to **Jesus** (saw) has been recorded in this hadith-like book is unknown.

According to the **Rasul of Allah** (saw) one may pray wherever and whenever they like without having to put anyone in between themself and Allah! One is not bound by any *fatwa*, mufti, *haji*, *hodja* or sheikh! Then, turn to **Allah in your essence** wherever and whenever you remember and ask everything of Him! You do not need to follow any of the hundreds of thousands of *fatwas* released by the tens of thousands of *hodjas* to date!

Fatwa, in religion, is not an institution; it doesn't bind anyone. It is merely a personal interpretation; in fact, if the interpreter is mistaken, his *fatwa* will not be a valid excuse for you either.

Founding your life on the teachings of the **Rasul of Allah** (saw) is sufficient to attain eternal bliss.

My friend, if this era, which began in the 1400s, really is the final one... Then let us know that this is the period in which *mazhaps* and *tariqahs* will come to an end and the knowledge of the Reviver will disseminate throughout the world. This is the period when, in congruence with the knowledge of that honored one, from which I also benefit, the sun of the **Rasul of Allah** (saw) will shine bright and enlighten our houses. When that sun shines, all of the stars will gradually disappear.

But if, on the other hand, this isn't the era of the final Reviver but just the Reviver of this millennium... That is, is this period isn't the one preceding the Doomsday of humanity... If all of the signs of the Doomsday are false, and the *Dajjal* (Antichrist) and Jesus are not to appear within the following years... Then I guess the dispute and bickering between various *mazhaps* and *tariqahs* is to continue for some time more...

I will watch from my town until my days come to an end... The **Rasul of Allah** (saw) was 61 when he left **your world**, I do not know how much longer I will live after my 60th year... But life passes too quickly and we don't know when our final whistle will be blown.

We must, therefore, make the best of our lives by studying the **Quran**, pondering on why certain words were employed and others weren't, what do these words mean... Why is the word **Rasul** used is the Word of Testimony and not **Nabi**, for example... Why is the name *Rahman* used in reference to teaching the Quran and not *Rahim* or *Haq*? If such significant words are not used in their original then your translation is inadequate in duly giving the message of the **Quran**.

Enter **through the door of Rasulullah** if you want **to reach Allah**! If you follow others, who refer you to the skies, to the God in their imagination, and try to sell the keys to heaven, you will squander your life in pursuit of a god in space, or some place beyond and outside of you, and then hopelessly deny his existence because you are unable to find him!

The ball is in your court, my friend!

Leaving the path of the **Rasul of Allah** (saw) for the path of *hajis* and *hodjas* will have no benefit for you on the day when all of the *hajis*, *hodjas*, sheiks and saints will be busy trying to save their own souls! Protect yourself from a day in which regrets will be of no use! **Reform your life! Reform your understanding of religion!**

My dear friends...

After sharing the knowledge Allah has bestowed me for over 40 years since my first book in 1965, I now see that many of the concepts I introduced are now being embraced by many groups, from the fundamentalists to the new-agers and intellectualists, even if I am not referenced. I would like to share a final message with all the sincere and genuine researchers of religion:

If you sincerely embrace the religion of Islam, put aside the interpretations of yesterday, bound by yesterday's conditions and life standards, and re-construe the knowledge passed down by **Muhammad** (saw) in the light of what today offers!

There is no such thing as reform in religion! For religion is solidly founded upon the unhanging foundation of *sunnatullah*.

Religion is the universal system of Allah; it is impossible to reform it! Just as you cannot change the mechanics of your body, or the laws of nature, the universal laws called religion are also unalterable. The reform must take place in your own understanding; one must reform his life by re-learning the **religion of Islam Muhammad** (saw) **taught**.

A reform in understanding religion has already started to take place in our century. I am not referring to the localized efforts implemented by various communities. Such approaches are meaningless, religious groups or councils trying to reform religion by congregational attempts can never bring a true reform. What I am talking about is a complete reconfiguration of our understanding of religion by revising it from the beginning.

Any alleged reform based on a 'heavenly god and his postman-prophet on earth' approach will be too absurd to be considered by any intellectual person!

Any and all methods that neglect the spirit of the Quran can offer nothing but nonsensical and literal approaches going no further than the shapes and forms of the letters comprising god's literal book of commands! Consequently, they will be reinforcing the deficient judgment 'faith is for the unintelligent' adopted by some shortsighted ones.

Islam was not delivered by a prophet with a stick, who came to chastise some tribe or clan, and instill in them the belief of a deity-god!

The religion of Islam is the religion of Allah; the only prescription of salvation for humanity! It is the disclosure of the dimensional system of the universe, as far as it concerns man. Though this is inconceivable for the shortsighted ones!

In Turkey, sadly, even the most intellectual ones have not been able to re-evaluate the religion of Islam in the light of science and in congruence with logic and intellect. Religion never seems to be evaluated with the questions what, why and how, instead the conditioned approach *'if such and such said it must be true'* is what generally seems to be applied. Localized solutions are futile. Like blind men holding various parts of an elephant, and each construing it to be something else!

We will get nowhere with the fiction '99% of the population is Muslim'! This is nothing but self-deception!

Let us be certain that **faith does not tolerate imitation**!

He who has not consciously comprehended the matters of faith can never be a true believer. Imitative attitudes will yield no benefit in the afterlife.

What the Muslims need more than anything is **knowledge**... Knowledge to elucidate the reality as it is, rather than a 'Reviver-*Mahdi*' and cookie cutter prescriptions for salvation!

Leave the past in the past, start a new day today. Make your aim to re-evaluate the teachings of the magnificent **Rasul of Allah, Muhammad** (saw), Allah's biggest blessing to humanity. This is not a difficult task. All one must do is to try to understand the **spirit** of his teachings, the **spirit of the Quran**.

I would also like to take this opportunity to clarify that reading only one of my books is not sufficient to comprehend the system I am referring to comprehensively. To understand my view one must read all of my books. For each one of them is like a single volume from a vast collection explaining the system and order of Allah denoted by the religion of Islam.

My view and understanding is transparently evident in all my works. I hope that you pray for this humble servant, that Allah blesses him with peace and faith and guides him to the path of **Rasulullah** (saw) despite all of his shortcomings...

Do not waste your time with my gossip, for if I am blameworthy I will assuredly suffer the consequences of my mistakes, but if I am of the righteous, then whatever you say will have no effect on me anyway, it will only waste your time and breath!

Besides, if my evaluations, all of which are based on the teachings of the **Quran**, the **Rasul of Allah** (saw), and the most eminent leaders of spirituality, are correct, then how much validity can opposing beliefs hold anyway? This I leave to your judgment...

May Allah save us from our conflicts and aid us to prepare a favorable future for ourselves!

Eid has come! The eid of Ramadan, the eid of offering thanks, eid for those who attained the prosperity of the month of Ramadan…

May your eid be blessed with the light of the **Rasul of Allah** (saw)!

If you get to know him and his purpose your love for him will strengthen, for he is closer to you than your close ones, and more protective over your than you can imagine. He has strived much too hard to enable a safe and blissful future for you! I pray this eid will be the eid of realizing this truth.

I pray that, for the sake of His beloved one, Muhammad Mustapha (saw), **Allah blesses this humble servant and anyone who has listened, shared and contributed to the distribution of this knowledge, with the light of faith and ability, certainty (*yakeen*) of faith, and protection from all extremes!**

May the blessing of Allah be upon his Rasul in a way most suited to His knowledge!

May Allah guide us all to the proper evaluation of Islam, as disclosed by the Rasul of Allah (saw).

I wish you clarity in mind and thought and apologize for any transgressions from my behalf, if there has been any, I hope that you find forgiveness and tolerance in your heart …

May the guidance of Allah be with you always.

Farewell, my friends…

3 November 2005
Expo channel conferences

42

SELECTED VERSES FROM THE BOOK OF ALLAH

1. "'O you who have believed; *Aminu B'illahi*[32]' That is, 'O you who have believed, believe in Allah in accord with the meaning signified by the letter B.'..." (Quran 4:136)

2. "And of the people are some who say, 'We believe in Allah (in accord with the meaning of the letter B – that His Names comprise our being) **and the life after'** (that we will forever live the consequences of our deeds), **but they are not believers** (in accord with the meaning of the letter B)." (Quran 2:8)

3. "**So believe in Allah, whose Names comprise the essence of your being, and his Rasul, the Ummi Nabi, who believes in Allah, the essence of his self, and what He disclosed...**" (Quran 7:158)

4. "**As for those who believe in Allah, the essence of everything, and hold fast unto Him as their essential reality –**

---

[32] What does this mean? It means: Among all the worlds that are constituted by the meanings of the Names of Allah, your reality, existence and being also comprise the Names of Allah. Your Rabb, your very Reality is the al-Asma (the Names). Therefore, neither you nor anything else around you is anything other than the manifestations of these Names. So do not be of those who fail to see this non-dual reality, and who give a separate existence to things (like God) they believe is 'other' than Allah. Such duality will only result in burning, both in this life and the next. For further information: *Introductory Information to Understanding the Quran*

HU will admit them to grace (*rahmah*) **and bounty** (the awareness of the qualities of the Names) **and guide them to Himself** (enable the observation of their innermost essence) **on a straight path** (*sirat al-mustaqim*).***"*** (Quran 4:175)

5. **"And when it is said to them, 'Believe what Allah has revealed** (the knowledge that the Names of Allah comprise the entire existence, your very being and the knowledge of *sunnatullah*),**' they say, 'No, rather, we will follow that which we found our fathers following** (external deification).**' What if their fathers were misguided and failed to understand the reality?"** (Quran 2:170)

6. **"...Verily Allah is *Ghani* from the worlds** (in terms of His Absolute Essence, Allah is free from being conditioned and limited by the manifested compositions of His Names).***"*** (Quran 29:06)

7. **"...There is nothing that resembles HU!..."** (Quran 42:11)

8. **"Every constructed sense of self** (ego) **on the earth** (corporeal life) **is illusory** (inexistent). *Al-Baqi* (eternal, without being subject to the concept of time) **is the face** (absolute reality) **of your *Rabb*** (the meanings of the Names comprising your essence), **the *Dhul-Jalali Wal-Ikram*."** (Quran 55:26-27)

9. **"Sensory perception perceives Him not but He perceives** (evaluates) **all perception..."** (Quran 6:103)

10. **"...Never can '*You*'** (with your illusory self – ego) **see** (comprehend) **'*Me*'...** (Absolute Reality, Absolute 'I')..." (Quran 7:143)

11. **"They did not justly appraise** (the manifestations of the qualities denoted by the name) **Allah ..."** (Quran 22:74)

12. **"*Rahman* is established on the Throne"** (*Rahman* established His sovereignty by creating the worlds [the existential world created by the potential of the Names inherent in one's brain] with His Names, i.e. *Rahman* observes His knowledge with His knowledge, in the quantum potential)." (Quran 20:5)

13. **"Verily, when He wills a thing, His Command is, '*Kun* = be'** (He merely wishes it to be), **and it is** (formed with ease)! *Subhan* **is He in whose hand** (governance) **is the *Malakut*** (the

force of the Names) **of all things, and to Him you will be returned** (the illusory self – ego will come to an end and the Absolute Reality will be discerned)." (Quran 36:82-83)

14. **"Within your own selves** (the essence of the self). **Will you still not see** (discern)**?"** (Quran 51:21)

15. **"And whoever is blind** (unable to perceive the truth) **in this life** (outer life) **will also be blind in the eternal life to come** (inner life) **and further astray in way** (of thought)**."** (Quran 17:72)

16. **"HU is the *Al-Awwal*** (the first and initial state of existence) **and *Al-Akhir*** (the infinitely subsequent One, to all manifestation)**, *Az-Zahir*** (the explicit, unequivocal and perceivable manifestation; the Absolute Reality beyond the illusion) **and *Al-Batin*...** (the unperceivable reality within the perceivable manifestation, the source of the unknown; the Absolute Self beyond the illusory selves) (There is nothing other than HU)." (Quran 57:3)

17. **"...We are closer to him than his jugular vein** (within the dimensions of the brain)**!"** (Quran 50:16)

18. **"...And He is with you** (the origin of your being) **wherever you are** (as your reality exists with His Names)**...** (This points to the unity of existence beyond the illusion of duality)." (Quran 57:4)

19. **"...So wherever you turn, there is the face of Allah** (you are face to face with the manifestation of the qualities denoted by Allah's Names)**..."** (Quran 2:115)

20. **"...Be careful! Verily He is *Al-Muhit*** (the One who forms the existence of all things with the qualities of His Names)**."** (Quran 41:54)

21. **"...Fear me** (for you will face the consequences of your deeds based on the mechanics of the system; *sunnatullah*)**, if you are of the believers."** (Quran 3:175)

22. **"...Which will tell them that man had *no certainty* in Our signs** (they were unable to observe the qualities of the names that comprise their being)." (Quran 27:82)

23. **"...Verily, if you follow their desires** (ideas and wants formed by their conditionings) **after what has come to you of**

knowledge be among the wrongdoers (those who punish themselves as a result of their failure to discern their essential reality)." (Quran 2:145)

24. "Set your face (consciousness) as a *Hanif* (without the concept of a deity-god, without making *shirq* to Allah, i.e. with the consciousness of non-duality) towards the One Religion (the only system and order), the natural disposition (*fitrah*) of Allah (i.e. the primary system and mechanism of the brain) upon which Allah has created man. There is no change in the creation of Allah. This is the infinitely valid System (*deen al-qayyim*) but most people do not know." (Quran 30:30)

25. "And We have created the heavens (the stages of manifestation pertaining to the qualities denoted by the Names) and earth (man's illusory world) and everything in between them in Absolute Truth." (Quran 15:85)

26. "... Say: 'Allah' and let them amuse themselves in their empty discourse (their illusory world) in which they're absorbed." (Quran 6:91)

27. "...And you threw not, when you (illusory self; ego) threw, but it was Allah who threw..." (Quran 8:17)

28. "He is not questioned for what He does! (as there is no duality!)..." (Quran 21:23)

29. "...He creates whatever He wills..." (Quran 42:49)

30. "...Indeed, Allah does as He wills (He forms what He wills to manifest from His knowledge with Power; Knowledge – Will – Power)." (Quran 22:14)

31. "...Allah does as He wills (Allah manifests the qualities of His Names that He wishes!)." (Quran 14:27)

32. "...Allah enables the observation of his innermost essential reality to whom He wills." (Quran 22:16)

33. "...Allah (the Names [the various compositions of structural qualities constituting existence] within the essence of man) enables the realization of His *Nur* (the knowledge of the Absolute Reality beyond what is perceived) whom He wills." (Quran 24:35)

34. "Whoever Allah enables the observation of his innermost essential essence, he is the one who reaches the reality..." (Quran 7:178)

35. "He who Allah enables the observation of his innermost essential reality can never be led astray!..." (Quran 39:37)

36. "...Allah enables those who turn to Him to realize their inner reality!" (Quran 42:13)

37. "He gives wisdom (the system by which the qualities of the Names are manifested) to whom He wills, and whoever has been given wisdom has certainly been given much benefit. And none will discern this except those with intellect and deep contemplative skills." (Quran 2:269)

38. "Allah chooses (enables the comprehension of one's inner reality) for Himself whom He wills..." (Quran 42:3)

39. "...Such is the bounty of Allah (the realization of the vastness of the qualities of the Names), which He grants unto whomever He wills..." (Quran 57:21)

40. "And whomsoever Allah wills the realization of his essential reality, He opens his breast (his innermost comprehension) to Islam (to the consciousness of his submission) and whomsoever He wills to lead astray, He makes his breast tight and constricted, as though he were laboriously climbing into the sky!..." (Quran 6:125)

41. "...but Allah purifies (from the illusory self; ego) whom He wills..." (Quran 24:21)

42. "He who purifies (his consciousness) has succeeded." (Quran 91:9)

43. "...Know well, that (if you do not attend to this invitation) Allah will intervene between the person's consciousness and his heart (Allah creates a barrier between his emotions and reason, abandoning him to an emotional state of existence that comprises his hell through the system of the brain) and prevent him. To Him you will be resurrected (you will reside in a realm in which the Absolute Reality will become apparent; you will be evaluated by the qualities of the names that comprise your essence)." (Quran 8:24)

44. "**...Every instance HU** (the Absolute Essence of Existence) **manifests Himself in yet another way.**" (Quran 55:29)

45. "**Allah abolishes what He wills or forms** (into a perceivable reality, what He wills)**, and with Him is the Mother of the Book** (primary knowledge; the knowledge of the ways in which the Names will manifest at every instant)." (Quran 13:39)

46. "**My decision** (rule) **will not be altered!...**" (Quran 50:29)

47. "**...And Allah gives provision** (both limited sustenance for the corporeal life and infinite life sustenance pertaining to the realization of one's inner reality and its benefits) **to whom He wills without account.**" (Quran 2:212)

48. "**...To each of you We prescribed a law** (rules and conditions regarding lifestyle) **and a method** (a system based on fixed realities not subject to change within time)**...**" (Quran 5:48)

49. "**The Rasul** (Muhammad (saw)) **has believed in what was revealed** (knowledge that emerged from the dimensional depths) **to him** (to his consciousness) **from his Rabb** (the qualities of the Names of Allah comprising his essential reality)." (Quran 2:285)

50. "**...We make no distinction between** (the ways in which the knowledge of Allah was revealed to) **His Rasuls...**" (Quran 2:285)

51. "**...Had Allah willed, He would surely have enabled the realization of the absolute reality to all of mankind...**" (Quran 13:31)

52. "**And if We had willed, We could have enabled every being** (illusory self; ego) **to realize its essential reality, but My word: 'I will surely fill Hell** (the conditions to manifest the specific configuration of the qualities of the Names that result in an infernal state of life) **with *jinn* and man all together' is in effect.**" (Quran 32:13)

53. "**Had your *Rabb*** (the reality of the Names comprising your essence) **willed, all those who live on earth would surely have had faith** (in the qualities of the Names of Allah that comprise his being and all that is manifested through him)**, all of them entirely... So then, will you compel the people to become believers? And it is

not for a soul to believe unless the unique composition of Allah's Names comprising his essence permits." (Quran 10:99-100)

54. "**No more is the Rasul bound to do except to provide the knowledge** (of the reality and its requisites)..." (Quran 5:99)

55. "**There is no compulsion in** [acceptance of] **the religion** (the system and order of Allah; *sunnatullah*)..." (Quran 2:256)

56. "...**and never will suffering occur unless a Rasul of the absolute reality is revealed.**" (Quran 17:15)

57. "**And We have not revealed you except as grace to the worlds** (people)." (Quran 21: 107)

58. "...but [he is] **the Rasul of Allah, the final of Nabis** (the summit of perfection)." (Quran 33:40)

59. "**O covered one; arise and awaken!**" (Quran 74:1-2)

60. "**Say** (O Rasul): '**I am only a man like you** (aside from the knowledge of Allah disclosed through me [*Risalat*], we possess the same reality).'" (Quran 18:110)

61. "**And obey Allah and His Rasul...**" (Quran 8:46)

62. "**Indeed, the religion** (system and order) **in the sight of Allah is Islam** (the whole of creation is in a state of submission, whether conscious or unconscious of the qualities of the Names)..." (Quran 3:19)

63. "**And whoever seeks a religion** (system and order) **other than Islam** (the consciousness of being in a state of submission) **his search will be ineffective!** ..." (Quran 3:85)

64. "**Whose heart** (essence) **Allah has expanded towards comprehending Islam, is he not upon a *Nur*** (knowledge) **disclosed by his *Rabb*** (his essential reality)? ..." (Quran 39:22)

65. "**This day I have perfected for you your religion** (your acquisition of religious knowledge) **and completed My favor upon you and have approved for you Islam** (complete submission to Allah) **as** (the understanding of) **religion...**" (Quran 5:3)

66. "**It is HU who shapes** (forms, programs) **you in the womb** (mother's womb – in Arabic *rahim*; the productive mechanism within your essence: *rahimiyyah*) **as He wishes...**" (Quran 3:6)

67. "**...But if good comes to them, they say, 'This is from Allah'; and if evil befalls them, they say, 'This is from you.' Say, 'All [things] are from Allah...'**" (Quran 4:78)

68. "**Your *Rabb*** (reality of the Names comprising your essence) **creates and chooses as He pleases, they have no free will** (or choice)**...**" (Quran 28:68)

69. "**Who brings the living** (the consciousness of being alive with the Names of the *Hayy*) **out of the dead** (the futile state of corporeal existence) **and brings the dead** (the state of being blinded to the reality of one's self or the reality of others; confining one's existence only to the body and assuming life is going to end once the body deteriorates under the soil) **out of the living** (while in respect of his essential reality he is alive)? **Who carries out the judgment? They will say, 'Allah'...**" (Quran 10:31)

70. "**...And whoever is grateful, his gratitude is for his self** (the realization and evaluation of the perfection of his essence)**...**" (Quran 27:40)

71. "**When a [single] disaster struck you, although we had struck [the enemy] with one twice as great, you said, 'Why and how did this come about?' Say, 'It has come about from yourselves** (your ego)'. **Indeed, Allah is *Qadir*** (the possessor of continual and infinite power) **over all things.**" (Quran 3:165)

72. "**...He who submits to, and places his trust in Allah, Allah will be sufficient for him** (he who believes in the forces pertaining to the qualities of the Names comprising his essence and complies with their requirements, those forces will be ever sufficient for him)." (Quran 65:3)

73. "**...Seek the continual manifestation of the Names of Allah** (from your essence in respect of its *Uluhiyyah*; from the forces of the Names comprising your being) **and have patience...**" (Quran 7:128)

74. "And your *Rabb* has decreed that you serve only Him (He created you to manifest the qualities of His Names)..." (Quran 17:23)

75. "I have created the *jinn* and men only so that they may serve Me (by means of manifesting the qualities of My Names)." (Quran 51:56)

76. "He is *al-Badee* (The originator of the heavens [states of consciousness] and the earth [the body] who makes things without any sample or like). **When He wills a thing, He only says to it, 'Be,' and it is.**" (Quran 2:117)

77. "...While it is Allah who created you and all your doings." (Quran 37:96)

78. "Do you not see that to Allah prostrates whoever is in the heavens and whoever is on the earth, the sun, the moon, the stars, the mountains, the trees, the moving creatures and many of the people? But upon many the suffering has been justified. And he whom Allah humiliates – for him there is no bestower of honor. Indeed, Allah does what He wills." (Quran 22:18)

79. "Say: 'Everyone acts according to his own creation program (natural disposition; *fitrah*).'..." (Quran 17:84)

80. "**And to Him belongs whoever is in the heavens** (conscious beings) **and the earth** (bodily beings). **Thus, all are in a state of devout obedience to Him** (in manifesting the qualities of His Names)..." (Quran 30:26)

81. "**...The seven heavens** (all creation within the seven dimensions of consciousness) **and the earth** (the bodies) **and whatever is in them *continue their existence through* Him** (*tasbih*). **And there is not a thing that does not continue its existence through His *hamd*** (the reality of the Names comprising one's essence [*Rabb*] is the evaluator of this continual existence), **but you do not understand their** [way of, discourse, disposition] **disclosure...**" (Quran 17:44)

82. "**...There is no animate creature but that He holds its forehead** (the brain; the very qualities of the Names of Allah!)..." (Quran 11:56)

83. "**You cannot will unless Allah wills** (your will is Allah's will)..." (Quran 76:30)

84. "**Indeed we have created everything with its program** (*qadar*)." (Quran 54:49)

85. "**And there is not a thing of which its depositories** (the forces comprising it) **is not with us! And We disclose** (the forces/qualities) **according to its program. The requirements of its core creation program unfold sequentially.**" (Quran 15:21)

86. "**No calamity befalls you on earth** (on your physical body and outer world) **or among yourselves** (your inner world) **that has not already been recorded in a book** (formed in the dimension of knowledge) **before We bring it into being! Indeed for Allah, this is easy. We inform you of this in order that you don't despair over your losses or exult** (in pride) **over what We have given you, for Allah does not like the boastful and the arrogant!**" (Quran 57:22-23)

87. "**...Perhaps you hate a thing and it is good for you; and perhaps you love a thing and it is bad for you. And Allah knows, while you know not.**" (Quran 2:216)

88. "**Whatever good comes to you it is from Allah, but whatever evil comes to you it is from your self** (from complying with your conditioned beliefs including your alleged 'moral codes')..." (Quran 4:79)

89. "**...Indeed, the *dhikr*** (remembrance) **of Allah is Akbar** (enables one to experience *Akbariyyah* – Absolute Magnificence)..." (Quran 29:45)

90. "**...and engage much in the *dhikr*** (contemplation on the forces of the Names comprising your essence) **of Allah so you can overcome difficulties and attain salvation.**" (Quran 8:45)

91. "**...And remember** (*dhikr*) **Him, to the extent of your awareness of your innermost essential reality...**" (Quran 2:198)

92. "**Allah will never hold anyone responsible for that which they have no capacity...**" (Quran 2:286)

93. "Remember (*dhikr*) the qualities of the Names comprising your essence; your *Rabb*, and seclude yourself to Him in complete devotion." (Quran 73:8)

94. "So remember (*dhikr*) Me; so that I will remember you." (Quran 2:152)

95. "...And remember Allah while standing, sitting, or [lying] on your sides (i.e. experience Him in your being at all times)..." (Quran 4:103)

96. "They (those who have attained the essence of the reality) remember Allah while standing or sitting or [lying] on their sides..." (Quran 3:191)

97. "And if you speak your thoughts (or conceal them,) know that indeed He knows the secret (in your consciousness) and what is [even] deeper (the actual Names that compose it)." (Quran 20:7)

98. "O believers! Let not your worldly goods or your children prevent you from the remembrance of Allah (the remembrance of your essential self and the resulting experience). And whoever does this – it is they who are the losers!" (Quran 63:9)

99. "And he who turns away from My *dhikr* (the absolute reality of which I have reminded him) indeed, he will have a restricted life (limited by the conditions of his body and mind), and We will resurrect him as blind on the day (period) of resurrection." (Quran 20:124)

100. "They (the objects/idols of their worship) will say, '*Subhan*, You are! It is not possible for us to take besides You any allies. But when You provided comforts for them and their fathers, they forgot the knowledge of reality and indulged in bodily pleasures eventually leading to their ruin.'" (Quran 25:18)

101. "...And whoever is blinded (with external things) from the remembrance of *Rahman* (remembering that his essential reality is composed of the Names of Allah and thus from living the requirements of this) We appoint for him a Satan (a delusion; the idea that he is only the physical body and that life should be lived in pursuit of bodily pleasures) and this (belief) will become his (new) identity! And indeed, these will avert them from the way [the

path to reality] **while they think that they are on the right path."** (Quran 43:36-37)

102. "Satan (corporeality; the idea of being just the physical body) **has overcome them and made them forget the remembrance of Allah** (their own reality of which they have been reminded, and that they will abandon their bodies and live for eternity as 'consciousness' comprised of Allah's names!) **Those are the acquaintances of Satan** (those who are receptive to satanic impulses and who think of themselves as only the physical body). **Beware, for most assuredly, the party of Satan will be the very losers!"** (Quran 58:19)

103. "[Are] men whom neither trade nor worldly dealings distracts from the *dhikr* of Allah (remembering their essential reality) **and performance of *salat*** (experiencing their essence) **and giving of *zakah*** (unrequited sharing)." (Quran 24:37)

104. "And when My servants ask you concerning Me – indeed I am Qarib (so close that you are naught; only I exist... Let us remember the verse 'I am nearer than the jugular vein'). **I respond to the one who turns to me and asks of Me** (in prayer)..." (Quran 2:186)

105. "...And never will you find in the System (course) **of Allah** (*sunnatullah*) **any change."** (Quran 48:23)

106. "...You will never see a change in *sunnatullah* (the mechanics of Allah's system)." (Quran 35:43)

107. "Maintain *salat* (prayer; turning to Allah) **with care [in particular] the middle *salat*** (*asr* prayer – the constant experience of this reality in one's consciousness)..." (Quran 2:238)

108. "So woe to those who pray (due to tradition)**, who are heedless** (cocooned) **of** (the experience of the meaning of) **their *salat*** (which is an ascension [*miraj*] to their innermost essential reality; their *Rabb*)." (Quran 107:4-5)

109. "They (the believers) **are awed by the experience of observing the qualities of Allah's Names."** (Quran 23:2)

110. "...Among His servants, only those who have knowledge (of what is denoted by the name Allah and who are aware of its

Might) **truly feel awe towards Allah!** (realize their nothingness in respect of His magnificence)..." (Quran 35:28)

111. **"Certainly, I have turned my face** (my consciousness), **cleansed from the concept of a deity** (*Hanif*), **toward 'Al-Fatir'** (He who creates everything programmed according to its purpose) **who created the heavens and the earth, and I am not of the dualists."** (Quran 6:79)

112. **"Did you not see the one who had deified his '*hawa*'** (instinctual desires, bodily form, illusionary self)..!" (Quran 25:43)

113. **"Indeed, Allah does not forgive** (apparent or discrete forms of) *shirq* (i.e. directly or indirectly assuming the existence of beings 'other' than Allah, whether external objects [apparent] or our own egos [discrete]; thereby fragmenting the non-dual reality), **but He forgives lesser sins other than this** (*ma doona*) ('lesser sins' here connotes the perception that actions are initiated by the self/ego rather than by Allah), **as He wills..."** (Quran 4:48)

114. **"...Certainly, if you live in a state of duality** (*shirq*), **all your doings would surely become worthless and you would surely become among the losers..."** (Quran 39:65)

115. **"We will cast fear into the hearts of those who deify their egos** (duality) **over the Names of Allah comprising their essence, and cover the absolute reality within, even though there is no evidence that their ego-identities actually exist! And their abode will be the fire..."** (Quran 3:151)

116. **"...Assuredly, duality is a great injustice/wrongdoing** (duality, which denotes the denial of one's essential qualities referenced as the Names of Allah, leads to one's deprivation from these core qualities)." (Quran 31:13)

117. **"Verily the dualists** (who claim the existence of their ego-identities alongside the Absolute Oneness) **are contaminated..."** (Quran 9:28)

118. **"...None but the purified** (from the dirt of *shirq* – duality – animalistic nature) **can touch it** (i.e. become enlightened with the Knowledge of the Absolute Reality)." (Quran 56:79)

119. "**Do not assume the existence of a god** (exterior manifestations of power or your illusory self) **besides Allah. For there is no God. Only HU! Everything** (in respect of its thingness) **is inexistent, only the face of HU** (only that which pertains to the Absolute Reality) **exists!...**" (Quran 28:88)

120. "**Do not make** [up in your mind] **another deity besides Allah** (do not deify your illusory selves)**! Lest you find yourself disgraced and forsaken** (as a result of your *shirq*, dualistic understanding, you will be confined to the limits of your ego rather than manifesting the infinite potential of your essence)." (Quran 17:22)

121. "**Allah knows with certainty that none exists other than He. He is HU, there is no other, only HU... and** (so do) **the forces** (potentials) **of His names** (angels; compositions of qualities that manifest through the knowledge of reality) **and those of knowledge** (those who possess this knowledge also know, and thus testify this reality) **and maintain themselves in accord with this truth...**" (Quran 3:18)

122. "**Had there been within both** (the heavens [meanings] and the earth [actions]) **gods besides Allah, verily this system would have lost its order. So exalted** (*subhan*) **is Allah, *Rabb* of the Throne** (who creates and forms existence from the quantum potential, at will) **beyond the definitions they attribute to Him.**" (Quran 21:22)

123. "**So magnificent is He Who forms constellations in the skies** (the materialization of the various compositional groups of His Names at the macro level)..." (Quran 25:61)

124. "**Indeed, We have adorned earth's heaven** (configured man's brain) **with planets** (astrological data) **and protected it from every rebellious Satan** (the purified consciousness is beyond the reach of illusory impulses)." (Quran 37:6-7)

125. "**...And the stars are subjected by and in service to His command** (the stars are also a manifestation of the meanings of the Names comprising their essence)..." (Quran 16:12)

126. "**He governs the earth** (the brain) **from the heaven** (through the cosmic electromagnetic energy emanating from the

qualities of the Names in the form of celestial constellations [star signs] that affect the second brain in the gut and thus one's consciousness, or from an internal perspective, through the Names that become manifest in one's brain based on the holographic reality)..." (Quran 32:5)

127. "Allah is He who has created seven heavens and of the earth, the like of them. [His] command continually manifests among them (astrological [angelic] influences that are also manifestations of Allah's names and their effect on creation)." (This verse should be contemplated upon in depth!) (Quran 65:12)

128. "And indeed it is HU who is the *Rabb* of Sirius (star)!" (Quran 53:49)

129. "And leads to the reality by the (Names comprising the essence of the) **stars** (the people of reality, the hadith: 'My Companions are like the stars; whoever among them you follow, you will reach the truth')...!" (Quran 16:16)

130. "Had there not been a time (*dahr*), **when the name of man was not uttered?** (What is the validity of a piece of ice in the vastness of the ocean? i.e. man was not yet manifest; he was the unmanifest within the dimension of the Names)." (Quran 76:1)

131. "And [mention] when your *Rabb* took from the children of Adam, from their loins (semen, genes), **their descendants and made them testify to themselves,** [asking them], **'Am I not your *Rabb*?' and they said, 'Yes, indeed we bear witness!'** [Of this we remind you] – **lest you say on the day of Resurrection, 'We were cocooned** (unaware of this knowledge) **of this'** (This refers to man being created upon the natural disposition of Islam)." (Quran 7:172)

132. "And they (the Rabbis) **ask you, [O Muhammad], about the spirit. Say, 'The spirit is under the command of my *Rabb*** (Amr; the manifestation of the Names). **And you have been given little of this knowledge'** (this answer is for the Rabbis who asked this question)." (Quran 17:85)

133. "I will make upon the earth (the body) **a vicegerent** (conscious beings who will live with the awareness of the Names)." (Quran 2:30)

134. "**And He taught** (manifested and programmed) **Adam all of the Names** (all potential pertaining to the Names)..." (Quran 2:31)

135. "**We have certainly created man in the best of forms** (with the qualities of the Names). **Then We reduced him to the lowest of the low** (to the/their world of conditionings)." (Quran 95:4-5)

136. "**Who created you, formed you** (created you with a program to form your brain, an individual consciousness and a spirit) **and balanced you** (the work process of your brain, consciousness and spirit)! **Whatever form** (manifestation of Names) **He willed for you, He configured your composition accordingly.**" (Quran 82:7-8)

137. "**By the self and the One who formed** (the brain), **and inspired it** (individual consciousness) (with discernment of) **its wickedness** (its capacity to be misguided from the Reality and the System) **and its righteousness** (protection)." (Quran 91:7-8)

138. "**And serve your *Rabb* until there comes to you the certainty!** (the observation that your identity or ego is an illusion and inexistent, and the only valid reality is the Names; that death is the realization of the absolute reality; the experience of the *Wahid'ul Qahhar*) (after this certainty, servitude to one's *Rabb* will continue as the natural outcome of this process)" (Quran 15:99)

139. "**And man will only accrue the results** (consequences) **of his own labor** (what manifests through him; his thoughts and actions, due to the trigger system)[33]**.**" (Quran 53:39)

140. "**During this period every individual consciousness will be requited for what he has done** (face the consequences of his deeds) **no injustice** [will be done] **in this time: verily, Allah instantly puts into effect the consequences of one's actions.**" (Quran 40:17)

141. "**...And you will not be recompensed except for what you did** (your own actions)!" (Quran 36:54)

---

[33] The trigger system

142. "...And Allah did not cause them to suffer, but it was they** (their constructed self, ego-identity) **who caused their own suffering."** (Quran 29:40)

143. "And there are ranks based on what they manifest, so they may be fully compensated for their deeds, without any injustice."** (Quran 46:19)

144. "Indeed, you will be tasters of the painful suffering. And you will not be recompensed except for what you did** (your own actions)**."** (Quran 37:38-39)

145. "This is the result of what your hands have put forth. Verily, Allah is never unjust to [His] servants** (Allah is not the cause of your dual perception; it is the ego or your constructed identity who attributes a separate existence to itself, hence causing duality [*shirq*] which leads to suffering)**."** (Quran 22:10)

146. "And this apparent and perceived worldly life** (the lowest state of consciousness) **is no other than an amusement** (a delusive diversion in relation to the real) **and a game** (in which we merely play our roles in the script)**!"** (Quran 29:64)

147. "Realize well that the life of this world is but an amusement and diversion and adornment and boasting to one another and competition in increase of wealth and children... The things pertaining to the worldly life are nothing but a delusion."** (Quran 57:20)

148. "And We will surely test you** (your state of duality, *shirq*) **with fear and hunger and a loss of wealth and lives** (the lives of those who are dear to you) **and the produce of your labor, but give good tidings to the patient** (those who refrain from reacting impulsively and wait to see how things will turn out)**."** (Quran 2:155)

149. "Never will you experience the essence of reality** (*albirra*) **until you unrequitedly give away from that which you love most..."** (Quran 3:92)

150. "...They follow only assumption and the illusory desires of their ego** (even though) **the knowledge of Reality has indeed

come to them from their ***Rabb*** (the reality of the Names comprising their essence).***"*** (Quran 53:23)

151. **"And they have no proof thereof. They follow only unverifiable assumptions, and indeed, never can assumption reflect the truth."** (Quran 53:28)

152. **"Your assumption about your *Rabb* has brought you to perdition, and you have become among the losers."** (Quran 41:23)

153. **"O you who have believed, avoid most assumptions** (guesswork about things of which you have no certain knowledge). **Indeed, some assumptions are an offence** (lead to or are an outcome of duality). **And do not spy on others** (do not inspect or inquire into the private matters of others out of curiosity) **and do not backbite. Would one of you like to eat the flesh of his dead brother? You would detest it! ..."** (Quran 49:12)

154. **"And for all people a specified term** (lifespan) **is set. So when the end of their time has come, they can neither delay it by a single moment, nor can they hasten it**[34]**."** (Quran 7:34)

155. **"Every individual consciousness will taste death** (life without a biological body will continue eternally)**..."** (Quran 3:185)

156. **"And never think of those who have been killed in the cause of Allah as dead. Rather, they are alive with their *Rabb* receiving provision** (from the forces pertaining to their innermost essential reality).**"** (Quran 3:169)

157. **"They will not taste death therein except the first death** (they will forever).**"** (Quran 44:56)

158. **"During that period** (the eternal life) **they will see that is as though they had not remained** [in the world] **except for an '*Ashiyyah*'** (the time it takes for the sun to set below the horizon) **or the period of twilight."** (Quran 79:46)

159. **"How can you deny that the Names of Allah comprise your essence** (in accord with the letter B)**? When you were lifeless** (dead; unaware of your essential reality) **and He brought you to life**

---

[34] The incapacity of the people to discern the Nabi does not render the Nabi ineffective, but rather, suggests the end of the comprehension of that populace.

(with the knowledge He disclosed to you); **again He will cause you to die** (from the state of thinking you are only the body), **and again He will bring you to life** (purify you from confining your existence to your body and enable you to live in a state of consciousness)... **Eventually you will see your reality!**" (Quran 2:28)

160. "**And Allah causes you to grow from the earth gradually like a plant** (the body that comes from the earth continues its life as consciousness). **Then He will return you into it and again extract you from it. And Allah has made for you the earth an exhibition** (living environment), **so that you may traverse therein, on spacious ways.**" (Quran 71:17-20)

161. "**So when death finally comes to one of them, he says, 'My *Rabb*, send me back** (to worldly life) **so I may do what is necessary for my eternal future** (i.e. a faithful life which I did not heed or give importance to; the potential that I did not use and activate).' No!** (It is impossible to go back!) **His words are useless!** (His request is unrecognized in the system) **and behind them is a barrier** (an isthmus, a difference of dimension) **until the Day they are resurrected** (they cannot go back; reincarnation, being re-born for another worldly life is not possible!). **So when the Horn is blown** (when the process of resurrection, i.e. a new beginning, commences), **no relationship** (worldly interactions, family relations, titles or familiar faces) **will there be among them that Day, nor will they ask about one another** (in terms of earthly relations)." (Quran 23:101)

162. "[It will be] **during the period the earth** (the body) **will be replaced by another earth** (another body), **and the heavens as well** (individual consciousness will also be turned into another system of perception)..." (Quran 14:48)

163. "**They will murmur among themselves, 'You remained** (in the world) **only ten [hours].'**" (Quran 20:103)

164. "[It will be said], '**You were certainly in unmindfulness of this** (you were living in your cocoon), **and We have removed from you your veil, so your sight, from this period on, is sharp.**'" (Quran 50:22)

165. "**READ the knowledge** (book) **of your life! Sufficient is your self** (your consciousness) **against you at this stage as an accountant** (witness the results of your thoughts and actions during your worldly life lest you judge others)." (Quran 17:14)

166. "**If you could but see when they are confronted with the fire** (suffering) **they will say 'Oh, if only we can go back** (to our biological life on earth; as biological life is required to activate the forces within the brain) **and not deny the signs of our *Rabb*** (our intrinsic divine qualities and potential deriving from the Names that comprise our essential reality) **and be among the believers. But that which they concealed before** (the knowledge of reality with which that had been endowed) **has now become apparent to them. And even if they were returned they would return to the things from which they had been forbidden, they are liars indeed. And they say, 'There is none but our worldly life, and we will not be resurrected, if you could but see when they will be made to stand before their *Rabb*** (when they recognize and become aware of the potentials of the Names within their own reality). **He will say, 'Is this not the Reality?' They will say, 'Yes, it is our *Rabb*.' He will then say, 'So taste the punishment now as the consequence of denying the knowledge of reality.**" (Quran 6:27-30)

167. "**And that Day** (period) **Hell will be brought** (to enclose the earth) – **during this period man will remember and think, but what benefit to him will the remembrance** (*dhikr*) **be** (when he no longer has a body – brain with which he can develop his spirit)**?" He will say "I wish I had done beneficial things** (raised my consciousness level to observe the Names)." (Quran 89:23-24)

168. "**Indeed, Hell has become a place of passage** (everyone will pass from it)." (Quran 78:21)

169. "**And there is none of you who he will not encounter** (experience) **hell. This is, by your *Rabb*, a definite decree. Then We will save those who protected themselves** (who exhibit the forces that become manifest as a result of living ones reality) **and leave the transgressors on their knees!**" (Quran 19:71-72)

170. "**When they are shown to each other... To save themselves from the punishment of that period, the guilty ones**

will want to offer their sons to the fire in their stead... And his wife and his brother; and his nearest kindred who shelter him and everything on earth so that it could save him!" (Quran 70:11-14)

171. "Indeed we have warned you of a close suffering (caused by the realization of the truth through the experience of death)! On that day, man will observe what his hands have put forth, and those who denied the knowledge of reality will say 'Oh, how I wish I was dust!'" (Quran 78:40)

172. "On that Day the (hypocrite) men and two-faced women will say to those who believed, 'Wait for us that we may acquire some of your light (*nur*; knowledge of reality).' It will be said, 'Go back and seek light.' And a wall will be placed between them with a door, its interior (inner world) containing grace, but its exterior is torment** (the condition of those who fail to experience the reality is suffering, whereas observing the qualities of the Names leads to a state of grace)." (Quran 57:13)

173. "[On] the Day (during that period) Allah will not disgrace the Nabi and those who shared his faith. Their light (*nur*) will proceed before them and on their right; they will say, 'Our *Rabb*, perfect our *nur* (increase the scope of our observation) and forgive us...'" (Quran 66:8)

174. "So Allah conferred favor upon us and protected us from the suffering of the (hellfire; the state of burning) *samum* (an infusing microwave radiation that is harmful to the astral body)!" (Quran 52:27)

175. "In the sight of your *Rabb* (the perception at the level of your essential reality manifested by the forces comprising your being) one day is like one thousand (earthly) years! (Allah knows best but I believe this verse is in reference to the perception pertaining to the dimension of life after death, for, 'your *Rabb*' connotes the state of consciousness [the perception of time in one's brain or cocoon reality] as a result of one's *individual Rabb* or composition of Names. This is not in reference to the '*Rabb* of the worlds')" (Quran 22:47)

176. "**The angels and the Spirit will return to their essence in a period** (which will seem to you to be) **of fifty thousand years** (the period of time to reach Allah in their essence)." (Quran 70:4)

177. "**READ** (grasp) **with the Name of your *Rabb*** (with the knowledge that comprises your being)**, who created. Created man from *alaq*** (a clot of blood; genetic composition)**. Read! For your *Rabb* is *Akram*** (most generous)**. Who taught** (programmed the genes and the essential qualities) **by the Pen.** (That is) **Taught man that which he knew not.**" (Quran 96:1-5)

178. "**...And say to those who were given the knowledge of Reality – *sunnatullah*, and** [to] **the unlearned** (those who are ignorant of this knowledge; the dualists)**, 'Have you accepted Islam?' And if they submit to this understanding they are on the right path; but if they turn away – then upon you is only the** [duty of] **notification...**" (Quran 3:20)

179. "**And you did not recite any scripture** (like the Torah and the Bible) **before** (the KNOWLEDGE we disclosed)**, nor did you inscribe one with your right hand** (hence, he may be literate in the general sense[35])**. Otherwise** (had you been reciting and inscribing) **the falsifiers would surely have had doubt.**" (Quran 29:48)

180. "**But this is an honored Quran in a preserved tablet** (*Lawh-i Mahfuz*; the unmanifest knowledge of Allah and *sunnatullah*)." (Quran 85:21-22)

181. "***Ha Miim*. By the Knowledge that clearly discloses the reality, indeed we have made it an Arabic Quran so that you might** (understand it and) **use your reasoning to evaluate it!**" (Quran 43:1-3)

182. "**...We have not neglected a single thing in the READable** (**Book**) **of the created existence!...**" (Quran 6:38)

183. "**It is HU who has revealed to you the KNOWLEDGE** (**Book**)**; in which there are verses** [that are] **precise** (clear and net to understand) **– they comprise the foundation of the Knowledge** (**Book**) **– and others that are metaphoric** (symbolic expressions)**. As for those in whose hearts there is deviation** [from truth; ill

---

[35] See Quran 25:05

intent], **they will follow the metaphoric verses, interpreting them for the purpose of creating discord. Only Allah knows its [true] interpretation** [i.e. the exact messages these verses denote]. **But those firm in knowledge** (deep contemplators) **say, 'We believe in it. All [of it] is from our *Rabb*.' And no one can discern this except those who have reached the essence** (the enlightened ones with whom Allah hears, sees and speaks[36]).**"** (Quran 3:7)

184. "**And these examples** (symbolic language) **We present to mankind so they will contemplate.**" (Quran 59:21)

185. "...**And say 'My *Rabb*, increase my knowledge.'**" (Quran 20:114)

186. "...**To whom We had given** (gifted) **grace** (enabling him to experience his Reality) **and had manifested through him Our Knowledge** (the manifestation of divine attributes as the pleasing self [*nafs-i mardiyya*])." (Quran 18:65)

187. "...**Say, 'Can those who know be equal to those who do not know? Only those with deep contemplative intellects can discern this'**..." (Quran 39:9)

188. "**And your *Rabb* revealed to the bee**..." (Quran 16:68)

189. "**And there is no animate creature on** [or within] **the earth or bird that flies with two wings** (knowledge and power) **except** [that they are] **communities** (formed with an order based on a specific system) **like you!**" (Quran 6:38)

190. "...**Indeed, the grace of Allah is near the doers of good** (the grace of Allah reaches you by the hand that delivers it)." (Quran 7:56)

191. "...**The** (tree's) **oil** (the observation of the reality in consciousness) **would almost glow even if untouched by fire** (active cleansing)... **Light upon light!** (The individualized manifestation of the knowledge of the Names)..." (Quran 24:35)

---

[36] "When the servant approaches Me through his supererogatory acts, I love him, and when I love him I become his ears with which he hears, and I become his eyes with which he sees, and I become his tongue with which he speaks, and I become his hand with which he takes." (Hadith Qudsi)

The Essence of Man

192. "Indeed, we offered the Trust (living conscious of the Names) **to the heavens** (consciousness of the self, ego) **and the earth** (the body) **and the mountains** (the organs), **and they declined to bear it** (their Name compositions did not have the capacity to manifest it) **and feared it; but man** (the consciousness to manifest the Names that compose vicegerency) **undertook to bear it. Indeed, he is unjust** (insufficient in duly living his reality) **and ignorant** (of the knowledge of His infinite Names)." (Quran 33:72)

193. "And those who strive (against their egos) **to reach Us, We will surely enable them to reach Our ways** (by enabling them to realize their innermost essential reality... The ability to observe the manifestations of Allah's names ubiquitously). **Indeed Allah is with those who have certainty** (those who turn to Allah as though they see Him, i.e. the manifestations of the qualities of His Names)." (Quran 29:69)

194. "Except for those who have believed (in their essential reality) **and applied the requirements of their faith...**" (Quran 103:3)

195. "...Well-pleased is Allah with them, and well-pleased are they with Him (the reflections of divine qualities)..." (Quran 98:8)

196. "...And their *Rabb* will give them pure wine (the euphoric state caused by the exposure to the reality... all these descriptions pertaining to paradise, are similes and figurative representations as mentioned in verses 13:35 and 47:15. This should not be forgotten)" (Quran 76:21)

197. "The hue of Allah! And what can be better than being colored with the hue of Allah?" (Quran 2:138)

198. "And never will Allah fail to fulfill His promise." (Quran 3:9)

199. "As for he who gives (both *of* himself, i.e. his constructed identity, and *from* himself, i.e. from that which is valuable for him) **and protects himself, and believes** (confirms) **the Most Beautiful** (Names) (to be his essential reality), **We will ease him towards ease. But as for he who withholds and considers himself free of need** (of purification and protection) **and denies the Most Beautiful**

(to be his essential reality), **We will ease him toward the most difficult** (to a life veiled from the knowledge of the Reality and the *sunnatullah*)!" (Quran 92:5-10)

200. "...**Pilgrimage to the House** (Kaaba, the abode of Allah in one's heart) **is the right of Allah** (the qualities of the Names in one's essence) **upon all people who have the means to undertake it...**" (Quran 3:97)

201. "**Fight them;** (so that) **Allah will punish them through your hands and will disgrace them...**" (Quran 9:14)

202. "**You transform the night into the day, and You transform the day into the night; and You bring the living out of the dead, and You bring the dead out of the living. And You give provision** (both limited sustenance for the corporeal life and infinite life sustenance pertaining to the realization of one's inner reality and it's benefits) **to whom You will without account.**" (Quran 3:27)

203. "**Indeed We have created you, and given you form. Then We said to the angels, 'Prostrate to Adam** (in respect of Adam being the manifestation of the totality of Allah's Names)'; **so they all prostrated** (realized their nothingness in the sight of the manifestation of Allah's Names), **except for Iblis**[37]. **He was not of those who prostrated** (He was of the *jinn*; an ego based existence)." (Quran 7:11)

204. "**Thereupon Satan whispered suspicions to them** (to make them aware of their ego and corporeality)..." (Quran 7:20)

205. "**And he swore to them, 'Indeed, I am from among the advisors.'**" (Quran 7:21)

206. "**Thus he deceived them** (by imposing deluding thoughts, making them think they are the physical body; drawing their attention to their corporeality)." (Quran 7:22)

---

[37] Iblis is the name given to a specific *jinn*-based existence the lineage of which continues to serve the same function. The word Satan, on the other hand, is a symbol of reference to a state of existence driven by the ego and corporeality. Those who possess satanic attributes do not believe in an eternal life after the death of the physical body, and reject the knowledge that the Names of Allah comprise their essence.

207. "**And Adam disobeyed his *Rabb*** (succumbed to his ego), **and his way of life erred** (as a result of being veiled to the reality of the Names comprising his essence)." (Quran 20:121)

208. "**And Satan** (their ego) **had made pleasing to them their deeds and averted them from the** (righteous) **path... Though they were endowed with the ability to perceive the reality.**" (Quran 29:38)

209. "**And [mention] when We said to the angels, 'Prostrate to Adam,' and all but Iblis prostrated. He was of the *jinn*...** (thus in favor of his ego) **He disobeyed the command of his *Rabb*** (he did not have the knowledge of reality [the *jinni* have no apprehension of the knowledge of reality], they live purely by the ego. A.H.)." (Quran 18:50)

210. "**And recall when your *Rabb* said to the angels, 'Indeed I will create a human being from clay** (water plus minerals).' **So when I have formed him** (by programming his brain) **and breathed**[38] **into him** (became manifest to form the brain) **of My spirit. So the angels prostrated, all of them entirely. Except Iblis; he** (relying on his mind) **was arrogant and became of the deniers of the knowledge of Truth** (those who cannot recognize the essence/reality of others due to their egos)." (Quran 38:71-72-73-74)

211. "**[Allah] said, 'What prevented you from prostrating when I commanded you?' [Iblis] said, 'I am better than him. You created me from fire** (radiation – a specific frequency of wave. Note that the word fire [*naar*] in this verse is the same as the word used in reference to hellfire. This is worth contemplating upon! A.H.) **and created him from clay** (matter).' **[Allah] said, 'Descend from your rank, for this rank is not for arrogance and feeling superior over others. Go! Indeed, you have debased yourself.'"** (Quran 7:12-13)

---

[38] The word 'breath' which is '*nafh*' in Arabic literally means to blow out, i.e. to project explicitly, to manifest, to materialize.

212. "**[Iblis] said, 'Reprieve me until the Day they are resurrected** (after death).'" (Quran 7:14)

213. "**[Iblis] said, 'Because You have led me astray,** (*yudhillu man yashau* = based on the reality that He leads astray whom He wills), **I shall most certainly sit on Your straight path** (*sirat al-mustaqim*) **to prevent them. Then I will come to them from before them** (by provoking ambition in them and glorifying their sense of self [ego] to lead them to the denial of the truth) **and from behind them** (by imposing delusive ideas in them and leading them to disguised forms of *shirq* [duality]) **and on their right** (by inspiring them to do 'good deeds' that will take them away from You) **and on their left** (by beautifying misdeeds and making the wrong appear as right)... **And You will find most of them as ungrateful to You** (unable to evaluate what You have given them).'" (Quran 7:16-17)

214. "**[Iblis] said, 'I swear by your might** (the unchallengeable power within my essence denoted by the secret of the letter B), **I will surely mislead them all** (deviate them from spirituality, by making them confine their existence to their physical body and pursuing bodily pleasures). **Except, among them, who are pure in essence** (those to whom You have bestowed the experience of their essential reality).'" (Quran 38:82-83)

215. "**Allah has cursed** (Iblis) **for he had said, 'I will surely take from among Your servants a significant portion. And I will mislead them, and I will arouse in them** (sinful, bodily, empty) **desires, and I will command them so they slit the ears of cattle** (as sacrifice), **and I will command them so they will alter the creation of Allah.' And whoever takes Satan** (bodily temptations; ego) **as master instead of Allah has certainly suffered a great loss. Satan promises them and arouses false hope and desire in them. But Satan does not promise anything except delusion.**" (Quran 4:118-120)

216. "**And certainly, upon you is My curse** (separation from Me; inability to experience your essential reality, being trapped within your ego) **until the Day of Recompense** (the period in which the reality of the system will become clearly evident and thus experienced)." (Quran 38:78)

217. "[Allah] said, 'Descend (to the constricted lower state of bodily existence from a life governed by pure forces) **as enemies to one another** (the duality of body & consciousness)...'" (Quran 7:24)

218. "**You cannot turn** (those who are pure in essence) **against Him. Except he who is to enter the Hellfire.**" (Quran 37:162-163)

219. "**Verily Iblis proved his assumption** (regarding man) **to be correct, except for some of the believers they all followed him. And yet he** (Iblis/the *jinn*) **had no influential power at all over them! We only did this to reveal the distinction between those who truly believe in the eternal life to come and those who are in doubt thereof...**" (Quran 34:20-21)

220. "'**O communities of *jinn* and mankind, did there not come to you Rasuls from among you, relating to you My messages pointing to reality and warning you of the coming of this Day?' They will say, 'We bear witness against ourselves'; and the worldly life** (they had conjured based on corporeality) **had deluded them, and they will bear witness against themselves that they were deniers of the knowledge of reality.**" (Quran 6:130)

221. "**And the *jinn* We created before from '*samum*' fire** (an infusing microwave radiation that is harmful to the astral body)." (Quran 15:27)

222. "**And He created the jann** (the invisible beings, a type of jinn) **from a smokeless flame of fire** (radiation, radiant energy, electromagnetic wave body)." (Quran 55:15)

223. "**And** [mention, O Muhammad], **when We directed to you a group of the *jinn*, so that they may listen to the Quran. And when they were ready for it, they said, 'Be silent!' And when the provision came to place, they went back to their people as warners. They said, 'O our people, indeed we have heard a Knowledge revealed after Moses confirming what was before it which guides to the truth and to a straight path** (*tariq al-mustaqim*; knowledge that leads to the realization of one's servitude to Allah, with or without their consent) **O our people, respond to the DAI'ALLAH** (the *jinn* perceived him as the Dai'Allah not the **Rasulullah**; misused words such as 'messenger' denoting a courier

of information derive from this word) **and believe in him; Allah will forgive for you some of your sins**[39] **and protect you from a great suffering...'"** (Quran 46:29-31)

224. **"Our inadequate understanding has been making us claim foolish things about Allah! We had thought that mankind and the** *jinn* **would never speak a lie about Allah. And yet there were men and women from mankind who sought refuge in men and women from the** *jinn*, **thereby increasing** (provoking each other) **in excessive** (carnal) **behavior."** (Quran 72:4-6)

225. **"They turn to lifeless female deities in His stead, and hence they turn to none but stubborn useless Satan** (ego)." (Quran 4:117)

226. **"Indeed, they** (those who went astray) **had taken the satans** (the deviators) **as allies instead of Allah, and they consider themselves as rightly guided."** (Quran 7:30)

227. **"Yet they attributed the** *jinn* (invisible beings) **as partners onto Allah – while He** (Allah) **has created them** (the qualities they manifest are comprised of Allah's names)..." (Quran 6:100)

228. **"And we have appointed for them companions** (those with satanic ideas from amongst the *jinn* and man) **who made attractive to them their actions and desires. And the sentence concerning the** *jinn* **and man that had passed before them has now come into effect upon them. Indeed, they were [all] losers."** (Quran 41:25)

229. **"And they have assumed between Him** (Allah) **and the** *jinn* (conscious beings outside the human capacity of perception) **a connection** (i.e. associated divinity to them), **but the** *jinn* **know well that, verily, they** [who made such assumptions] **shall indeed be summoned** (will realize such a connection does not actually exist!)." (Quran 37:158)

---

[39] The forgiving of a sin means the elimination of the ego and the awareness that existence is none other than the manifestation of the Names.

230. "Indeed, he (Iblis and his lineage of *jinn*) **has no power over those who believe** (that their *Rabb* is sufficient) **and place their trust in their *Rabb*. His power is only over those who take him as a guardian** (who follow the ideas he imposes upon them) **and those who associate partners with their *Rabb*.**" (Quran 16:99-100)

231. "**The Day when He will gather** (resurrect) **them together** [and say], '**O community of *jinn*, you have truly possessed** (misled from reality) **the vast majority of mankind.' And their allies among mankind will say, 'Our *Rabb*, we mutually benefited from each other, and we have** [now] **reached our term, which you appointed for us.' He will say, 'The Fire is your residence, wherein you will abide eternally, except for what Allah wills...'**" (Quran 6:128)

232. "**Did I not enjoin upon you** (inform you), **O children of Adam, that you not serve Satan** (body/bodily and unconscious state of existence deprived of the knowledge of reality; ego driven existence) [for] **indeed, he** (this state of unconsciousness) **is to you a clear enemy! And that you serve only Me** (experience and feel the requisites of the reality), [as] **this is the straight path** (*sirat al-mustaqim*). **Verily, this unconscious state** (the assumption that you are merely the physical body prone to perish) **has already led astray most of you. Did you not use your reason?**" (Quran 36:60-62)

233. "**He called to his *Rabb*** (the reality of the Names comprising his essence), '**Indeed, Satan** (the feeling of being this body) **has given me hardship and torment.**'" (Quran 38:41)

234. "**And say, 'My *Rabb*** (the protective names within my essence), **I seek refuge in You from the incitements of the satans** (that call to corporeality). **And I seek refuge in You** (the protective names within my essence), **my *Rabb*, lest they be present with me.**'" (Quran 23:97-98)

235. "**O communities of *jinn* and mankind, if you are able to pass beyond the regions of the heavens and the earth, then pass** (live without a body!). **You cannot pass except by power** (the manifestation of Allah's power attribute on you). **So, this being the**

reality, which of the blessings of your **Rabb** (the reality of the Names comprising your essence – your consciousness and body) **will you deny? There will be sent upon** (both of) **you a flame of fire and smoke** (ambiguity and confusion in your consciousness), **and you will not be successful.**" (Quran 55:33-35)

236. "**And when** (during death) **the heaven** (the identity; the sense of self) **is split asunder and** (the reality) **becomes** (undeniably clear and the ego-self disappears) **burnt oil colored, like a rose**[40] (the reality is observed)**! So, this being the reality, which of the blessings of your Rabb** (the reality of the Names comprising your essence – your consciousness and body) **will you deny?**" (Quran 55:37-38)

237. "**Then on that Day none among men or *jinn* will be asked about his sin** (they will begin to live the natural consequences of their deeds)**!**" (Quran 55:39)

238. "**Certainly you will change dimensions and transform into bodies befitting those dimensions!**" (Quran 84:19)

---

[40] In Sufism, rose is the symbol of the observation of reality.

ABOUT THE AUTHOR

Ahmed Hulusi (Born January 21, 1945, Istanbul, Turkey) contemporary Islamic philosopher. From 1965 to this day he has written close to 30 books. His books are written based on Sufi wisdom and explain Islam through scientific principles. His established belief that the knowledge of Allah can only be properly shared without any expectation of return has led him to offer all of his works which include books, articles, and videos free of charge via his web-site. In 1970 he started examining the art of spirit evocation and linked these subjects parallel references in the Quran (smokeless flames and flames instilling pores). He found that these references were in fact pointing to luminous energy which led him to write *Spirit, Man, Jinn* while working as a journalist for the Aksam newspaper in Turkey. Published in 1985, his work called '*Mysteries of Man (Insan ve Sirlari)*' was Hulusi's first foray into decoding the messages of the Quran filled with metaphors and examples through a scientific backdrop. In 1991 he published *A Guide to Prayer and Dhikr (Dua and Zikir)*' where he explains how the repetition of certain prayers and words can lead to the realization of the divine attributes inherent within our essence through increased brain capacity. In 2009 he completed his final work, '*The Key to the Quran through reflections of the Knowledge of Allah*' which encompasses the understanding of leading Sufi scholars such as Abdulkarim al Jili, Abdul-Qadir Gilani, Muhyiddin Ibn al-Arabi, Imam Rabbani, Ahmed ar-Rifai, Imam Ghazali, and Razi, and which approached the messages of the Quran through the secret Key of the letter 'B'.

CPSIA information can be obtained
at www.ICGtesting.com
Printed in the USA
BVHW070228170520
579802BV00001B/75